From the Editor 2019

Pacific Daily Times Editorials

Jesse Steele

Amazon Paperback Edition

books.jessesteele.com

books@jessesteele.com

ISBN 979-8605055280

For MBI

Table of Contents

2019 Preface

My uncle used to warn me about China. For the record, he wasn't technically my *uncle*. Being my mother's cousin, he was my *first cousin once removed*. I say this to be factual and, so as not to digress, I shall simply call him my "uncle".

As I said, he used to warn me about China, long before I ever moved to Asia. This was twenty, even thirty years ago.

"China is a racist people," he would say. He never balanced his words with disclaimers because, being family, we all understood that he wasn't speaking about every single Chinese person in the world, but rather the thought that guided the nation of China today.

"In their mind, we are all less than human. They believe they are better than everyone else. And, they dream of a world where everyone is ethnically Chinese—the Chinese race. They won't stop until all other ethnicities are expunged and every country has only Han people with their Mandarin language. They are worse than the Nazis ever were and they are more determined."

Though I did not believe his words at face value, I did not forget them either. At the time, I just listened. I wasn't sure whether to believe him. He lacked proof, though he was a well-read, literate man, with even better command of the English language than my own mother and father.

Yes, I grew up in a family that used a large vocabulary. Yes, that probably contributed greatly to my own success in life. And yes, I'm getting a little off track, but not entirely.

While the words I just quoted are a paraphrase from my memories going back to my mid twenties, even early childhood, I grew up in a family that knew what words meant and how to use them. We knew how to learn about the world and how to explain what we learned.

So, I knew that clarity needed two things: I needed to heed my uncle's warnings, but first he needed evidence to both prove *and explain* what he meant. When I moved to Asia, I found that evidence all around me—from family to employment to Christianity to local idol worship to news and current events. Every day, Asia proved that my uncle was right.

Not everyone had the dark ideology he had described. No one had it fully, many had it little-to-none, but everyone in Asia I met behaved as if somehow marked by it.

How could I ever prove whether my uncle's warnings were factual? These warnings are not taught in a living, mainline education stream. Any evidence would be old and dusty and, thus, might have only represented but a fringe in history.

But, when we look at the nation China is ripening into—and with it the very culture that Hong Kong, Taiwan, many American-born Chinese, and other Westernized Chinese are working desperately to escape—we see living evidence that those dark ideologies may very well had been widely held many generations ago. That would be the best explanation of why things today became as they are.

Then, we have some direct claims from Chinese today—that China believes they are the center of the universe, that they are shameless in saying so loudly and often. Old school *Nationalists* from Chiang Kai-Shek's party, just before their political humiliation in Taiwan's 2016 elections, boasted about their superiority as having "Han" blood (from the Han Dynasty.)

I have my own testimony, having sat with members of the Chinese government when they visited my college in 2001. At dinner, they insisted that only a global government could end war. I asked if they wanted to run that government themselves; they were speechless. I then asked if they wanted America to run that government; they were adamantly opposed. I asked if they saw the dilemma of who would run a global government; they had never thought about that before. Their intentions were all too clear.

There are indeed some loud claimants proving that this ancient, dark ideology lives today—but they could be minority, so we ought not trust those witnesses alone as general proof.

As I stated, the primary evidence that the Chinese-supremacist ideology was widely-accepted long ago is its wide impact, evident in today's Eastern Chinese cultures and the nation China is maturing into, towering right before our eyes, printing presses, and blogs.

So, from a rumored, near-legend past, reasonably explaining and confirmed by our world today, China's ambitions should be no surprise. That's all I argue.

I won't claim that Chinese *people* are "bad" or "disgusting" or anything of the kind. I only report that my uncle had words that explain things all too well, all too far in advance. Because of my uncle, news stories don't surprise me either. Lack of surprise has always been the thesis of these editorials.

China is a conquering nation with a long history of "peace through tyranny". That is the theme of most Chinese history movies. By contrast, American history movies are about "life through liberty". Both require blood of patriots and tyrants. In American stories the patriots are the good guys because they bring freedom. In Chinese stories, the tyrants are the good guys because they impose peace.

Hitler said the world needed Germany. Xi says the same about China. As the trends indicate, China won't stop its "reclaiming" at the nine-dash line it printed around the South Sea in its passport page artwork. China won't stop at flying its Chinese flag above every nation in the world. No. The ancient ideology that drives Chinese expansionism—whether confessedly stated outright or only in deed—evinces that it will never halt until all other ethnicities are eradicated and the only remaining race in the world is Han. As with Germany, those most unaware may be the Chinese themselves.

It is absolutely essential that we understand the ideologies that drive us. Usually, we don't. The more we understand our past and present days, the less our futures will surprise us.

What, then, drives the English-West? Post Rome and as English speakers, our own aims at global conquest take a different form than the Chinese, but some kind of drive is apparent in that we either colonize or we "intervene and help" in such a way that establishes a long-term presence around the world.

The Spanish were partially similar; consider Latin America. Likewise consider Portugal with Brazil and Macau or the Netherlands with their Formosan colony, today known as *Taiwan.*

Most of Europe might be able to argue that the Biblical *Great Commission*—to "go into all the world... and make disciples from every nation..."—drives Western "expansionism".

But, English culture has a deeper, older history of conquest that predates the Bible's influence.

The peoples of the British Isles were conquered and compounded into being, thereby creating the English hybrid language itself, the youngest and yet most widely shared common language in human history.

English culture does carry a *noble habitus* of Bible-based, hardy servanthood, but also an ironic value set of independence mingled with conquest—though demonstrable, the origin of this odd value set remains silent. But, Chinese imperialism has a loud explanation.

Today, Far East and Far West are colliding. This is world-shaping history and it is happening in our time. So, pay attention.

While I remember the words of my uncle, I also know the words of the Bible. In college, Bible was my major. I know that war must come because of how messed-up we are as humans. But, I also know that war is not the end.

Now, I don't believe in a strange, conquest-driven worldview of "making a new world from the ashes of the old". I don't favor Pyrrhic victories—which purport it be "good" for the victor to become King of the Rubble.

My belief that war is "necessary" is that our human foolishness makes it inevitable, not that war should be invited, welcomed, or celebrated.

Quite the opposite! If we offer patience and explanation to those around us, war might become a little less inevitable, even avoidable. But, to have this insight, we must not only inform our worldview with ancient legends of evil, but also consider the Bible that foretold the good ending, nearly 2,000 years ago.

Foreseeability is my theme, though I pretend no special insight. It doesn't take a spy to know China's ambitions, only a historian. It doesn't take a psychic to know that war is coming—and with it victory—, only a Bible student. By studying the past, we know what the future is like; and by including the Bible, we know that the far future is surely bright.

Editor Notes

These articles were originally published to online readers on the dates indicated. They were collected and first made available in this printed format in early 2019. In this printed edition, they have neither been reviewed nor edited. While these articles aim to be useful and informative, as editorials, they are not news, but *comment* on the news, and never at any time have they, nor any part of this book, made any claim as to fact.

The names of various editorial series follow musical terms, hence they are collectively called *Symphony*.

The *Voice* series is a "think piece" analysis of current events and is often irregular.

The theme of *Prelude* is that a military conflict was on its way. When shots were fired over the Myanmar-China border, I decided that the prelude in Asia was ended and that the conflict had begun.

The theme of *Cadence* is that a military conflict marches on, evident and already present, though it may still seem orderly.

The theme of *Encore* is that good days of renaissance, revival, renewal, reconciliation, and revitalization of a nation and its people are clearly on their way. It is not only the song itself, but also the applause leading to it.

The *2019 Preface* was written just before this first became available in print. I had been accused of being pro-China by siding against Taiwan in these articles. Both before and after, I was told that I was responsible for stirring distrust of China among Taiwanese—regardless of poll data showing that China needed no help courting distrust on its own, especially in its own backyard. Though strange, I thought about both accusations deeply and reconsidered whether I had a bias. Indeed, I had been overly charitable. I thus conceived and wrote the *2019 Preface* as consequence. The editorials printed here were not influenced or guided by this *2019 Preface*, rather the *preface* was developed from history unfolding, which, upon self-review, demanded that the *preface* was credible.

Articles by Date

2019

Encore of Revival: America, January 7

Article IV Section 4 of the US Constitution states that the US government must "protect" each State from "invasion". It goes on to include protection from "domestic violence", but that requires action from the Legislature, unless the Legislature can't convene, then the Executive branch must take action.

It *does not* say, "The US government may protect the people if it wants to. And, if the Legislature refuses to, then the President must allow anyone and everyone to just destroy whatever they want to." It also *does not* say, "...unless they really, really want to come into the country, and that's why they're invading." But, that's how House Democrats would like to have it interpreted.

What's happening at the southern border is an "invasion"—people from the outside coming in by force. The Constitution *does not* specify that the invasion must be a sanctioned, deputized, funded military force operating at the behest of a recognized State. Any and every kind of invasion *must* be stopped, by Legislature or otherwise.

The Legislature is only required for situations of domestic violence. But, even then, if the Legislature can "convene"—and it can—but disobeys this Constitutional requirement, that could be cause for an action of impeachment because they would be in violation of their oaths of office, to support the Constitution. Then, the power to stop domestic violence would fall to the Executive branch, namely the president.

Trump is well within his powers to declare an emergency and take executive action, but he might be Constitutionally required to begin impeachment proceedings against Congress *if the border situation is regarded as domestic, not an "invasion" from non-US citizens.* So, claiming that Congress is needed to build the wall would actually be an argument to indite Congress.

As for citizenship by birth, that applies only to children of parents "subject to the jurisdiction thereof". Amendment XIV *does not* say, "Anyone can run from the police, sneak into the country, have a baby, then demand citizenship for that baby." But, that's how Congressional Democrats would like to have it interpreted.

The US is about to rediscover its Constitution, the document that united our nation at its founding.

That could redefine the entire playing field of elections in the future.

Cadence of Conflict: Asia, January 7

The US is working diligently to put Taiwan in the spotlight. It seems that Taiwan is being set up in the American public eye as the next Lusitania or Pearl Harbor—the punch that awakens the sleeping nation. It will be difficult, though, for an attack on foreign soil to provoke the public. That's where China seems to be playing on cue.

By wanting to sink a US Navy vessel, China would make the final push. Beijing doesn't understand American "exceptionalism"; it never has. Beijing doesn't know what freedom does to people, how much it energizes a threatened people. Americans won't respond as Chinese employees do to a boss who clears his throat; they will respond like William Wallace, just as they always do. But, when a nation isolates itself from Western free speech, that is difficult to know. We should expect China to *not* think that way.

Imagine China's perspective: Large US Navy carriers trouncing around the backyard, intimidating to the point that provoked China to the point we see now. To them, sinking a US Navy ship would seem like a big "shock" action because those carriers are the biggest American structure China can see. But, to American voters and soldiers, those carriers are across an ocean and are nothing compared to the size of achievements and monuments Americans see every day. So, China thinks a provocation would be an intimidation.

While it may take a US battleship to take a hit—God forbid—Taiwan will certainly be involved because that's the way the pieces are being set around the chessboard.

As for Xi Jinping and the Chinese, their resolve is absolute. Even pigs seem to be part of the attack on Taiwan.

A terminal disease specific to pigs seems to have swept Chinese pig farms. Taiwan has been going to great lengths to prevent Chinese pork from entering Taiwan for this very reason. This week, a dead pig with the disease floated ashore a Taiwanese island that sits just off China's coast. Panic is starting to set in throughout Taiwan—that a pork crisis could crash Taiwan's economy, cause the pro-US president to resign, making the perfect opportunity for China to invade. That's how the theories go, anyway.

The concern among Taiwanese is exactly the kind of response China anticipates from a "shock and awe" action against America. But, Americans are different than that, having both the "Wallace Complex" and a Congress-backed law that would compel a retaliation. Taiwanese have tasted some level of freedom, making the Taiwanese response as unpredictable as Taiwanese politics.

Encore of Revival: America, January 14

Pelosi and Schumer seem to be playing the Washington Generals, acting as if they are sincere, but not putting forward a formidable and convincing effort. Their resistance is a show and, by contrast to Trump, seems pathetic. It perfectly follows the tactic of "appearing to put up a fight". The most pathetic part is that they are probably sincere.

By standing side-by-side in their televised address, they appear to show unity between them, but the impression is that of weakness: it takes two legislators in order to respond to the president. More importantly, their rhetoric was weak. By mentioning that they would make a statement after his own address, the president positioned himself as the MC who facilitates discussion from all sides. For Democrats, the dual-address to the nation was a botched failure revealing no impression of the playbook sabotage it employed.

Trump is winning the government shutdown for one reason: he set a record. Senator Graham's desire to temporarily re-open the government was not a cave-in; it was proof of his desire to attempt cooperation of any kind. But, cooperation from Congressional Democrats doesn't seem likely since they are vacationing in Puerto Rico during the shutdown.

Trump's efforts to smooth relations with Russia can be interpreted from two perspectives: The first is from the one half of the masses who are suspicious of anyone who creates jobs without government. Those who don't understand how to create revenue see big and powerful people talking and—for that reason alone—presume themselves to be victims of some malevolent plot that may not even exist. The second perspective from which we may interpret the White House's policy with Russia is from the standpoint of the approaching conflict with China. The last thing the American people should want is Russia helping China takeover the Western Pacific. Thanks to Trump, that is unlikely. But, it's difficult to consider the Pacific factor for the narrow-thinking breed of voters whose primary political ambition is to vote themselves money from the Treasury.

But, they're about to learn, some of them anyway.

Cadence of Conflict: Asia, January 14

China is preparing for war. It has said so in public. It has demonstrated so with militarization of "Made in China" islands that didn't exist a decade ago. It has shown intent by showing no sense of limits in cyber-warfare, technology acquisition, and oppression of the press. Facebook and Twitter users are only a "security threat" to those easily threatened.

Unlike China, the United States does not make a habit of announcing its newest military technology to the world. Whatever warfare breaks out between the US and China in the Western Pacific, China's capabilities will have been known well in advance, but the US will likely employ weapons not yet known to the public. One needs no inside information to forecast as much, only a familiarity with the parts of history that tend to repeat.

But, we are not looking at WWIII, not yet. While the brewing conflict in the Western Pacific will likely involve many countries and islands, Russia is not yet ready for the big one. NATO's presence in Europe is still too strong and Putin has not had enough time to amass his forces as he would like.

Both Russia and the US would want things to quiet down rather quickly. Every effort from the White House to back away from conflicts with Russia suggests that a deal has already been struck with the Kremlin—that an expansionist campaign from China will not receive meaningful Russian help if squashed by the United States.

The question will concern how many Mainland China military supply installations Russia will allow the US to strike. But, if the US intervenes with Taiwan or razes the artificial islands on Mischief Reef, don't expect China to receive backup from Russia. Moscow took Crimea with a favorable referendum and no bloodshed. The Kremlin would expect just as much success from Beijing in order to court respect and cooperation. Right now, things don't look that way. 80% of Taiwanese rejecting reunification with China is a near flip to the support Russia received from Crimeans. Backroom Moscow secretly mocks Beijing, no matter how much money the Chinese pay them. Moscow would be fools if they didn't.

In the supposed "Chinese invasion plans" for Taiwan, there are multiple phases, including opportunistic retaliation from India. But, those plans fail to anticipate retaliation from the insulted Vietnamese, who also hold a long-standing grudge against China. Then, there is the ancient ethnic spite between China and Japan. Mongolia also has border disputes. Tibet is not the only province that wants to break away. It is doubtful Sun Tzu would have advised an expansion campaign while surrounded by enemies, especially as a mere means of being respected.

It would take a miracle and a half to stay whatever makes the pluming smoke on the horizon of the last decade. But, it won't last long. No one wants this to drag on. No, like "The Great War" (WWI) set the stage for WWII, the approaching war in the Pacific will set the stage for the big one that comes after.

Encore of Revival: America, January 21

Trump has transformed America's view of a "government shutdown" to a point where it could very well become a campaign promise in future elections. Not only did the shutdown become a "non-event", it's actually kind of nice to not have government messing with everything. If Congressional Democrats allow the shutdown to please Reagan Republican Americans much longer, political debates may even include strategy for how to keep the government closed for longer amounts of time.

It's difficult for Americans to sympathize with the purported "horror" of a government shutdown when the lives of hard-working Americans—*who work in the private sector*—continue their daily lives with little to no interruption. IRS agents being out of work won't be seen by Americans as a bad thing. If America's "tax collectors" hoped to get back to work sooner, they probably should have followed Biblical advice—to keep out of trouble by keeping their mouths shut. You'd think "IRS agents not working" should have been kept a State secret.

While those who depend on taxpayer dollars to fund their livelihood will be angry that the milk has run dry, the shutdown won't come close to affecting enough Americans to make a shutdown less popular in the future. In fact, the shutdown should prove to make America stronger on three levels: as a warning to government employees that the private sector is less likely to be destabilized by politics, that government and socialist -created "jobs" will eventually have the same problems in America as in North Korea, and that Americans will have to learn how to make due when government isn't operating in its greatest glory.

Look on the bright side. If America knows how to function without as much government, we will all get through tougher times with more colors flying.

Cadence of Conflict: Asia, January 21

The US government shutdown is stalling Beijing's action against Taiwan. With the US slightly less-able to respond and prepare, Beijing has an opportunity to bide time and grow its military. No doubt, Beijing will see advantage and seize opportunity.

At the same time, the US has zero intent of appeasing Beijing's hopes for Taiwan. Whatever signals the US sends elsewhere and otherwise, the US government shows no respect for China and China shows a slow learning curve on understanding just how little respect it has thus.

The evermore desperate fight inside Taiwan continues. Taiwanese rally around their defiant president. Taiwan's government is reaching for any friends it can find anywhere in the world, while policing dissidents and sources of pro-Chinese opinion within its borders. No doubt, Taiwan is headed for what Winston Churchill said of Great Britain, "this was their finest hour." Though history has not written the end of that hour, the time is fast approaching.

Encore of Revival: America, January 28

American deadlock trudges on. Trump promised a wall and he won't back down. Democrats won't back down either. Both show solidarity with their respective platforms. The only group that seems to favor backing down is Congressional Republicans, who want Trump to get this over with any way possible. For the compromising Republicans on Capitol Hill, Trump's refusal to sign a "wallless budget" isn't a "wall" strategy as much as it is a "shut down" strategy. Trump and Congressional Democrats see it differently.

Keep watch; it just might be Jared Kushner who saves the day.

The term "free speech" has taken a new meaning. While speech has kept less and less freedom from the tech bosses, the monetary cost of speaking out has essentially become free. With speech becoming more and more "financially free", the media industry can't find a way to stay solvent.

Newspapers and local news broadcasters seek collective ways to work against the tech giants, but they only rearrange their immediate problems with no long-term solutions in sight. The dwindling news industry is attacking "free" platforms of semi-free speech: social media. That's the clue of where news & information will head in the future.

Cadence of Conflict: Asia, January 28

The West ramped up rhetoric against China this past week. Even George "Socialist" Soros trashed the Chinese government, yet tried to court favor with the Chinese people. Such an attempt aims to divide government and people. Opinion pieces from renowned news outlets openly accuse China of aggression. We did not see such a harsh tone from the mainstream press in the West even one year ago. Today, it's becoming commonplace to bash China.

The US sent two Naval vessels through the Taiwan Strait this week. Now, the US is preparing extradition of the Huawei executive currently in Canadian custody. With threats of turning the tariffs back on, it should be more apparent that the US never planned to grant China any of its ambitions in the first place. Not only has the US been playing China like a flute, the Chinese haven't known—or have they?

Everyone seems to be biding time, both the US and China. China's main focus has been readying government and military. The US focus seems to have been public sentiment against China. Perhaps

both sides have been playing each other, but the
US has been making a play of its own—that we can
see.

Encore of Revival: America, February 4

Apple can crackdown on Google and Facebook, but America can't crack down on it's own private property and protection for citizens?

This week, the president's State of the Union Address will convene on schedule. The guest list is said to be interesting, though at press time, the president had not yet announced his guests. The regular speech is one way of fulfilling a Constitutional requirement that the president:

> ...shall from time to time give to the Congress Information of the State of the Union, and recommend to their Consideration such measures as he shall judge necessary and expedient.

The normal way of fulfilling this Constitutional requirement (the speech) was under threat by the government shutdown. That shutdown ended with a temporary budget, while Congressional Republicans proved that they saw "shutdown" as the strategy, while Congressional Democrats and President Trump—each in their own way—proved the shutdown as an unintended consequence of their "wall" or "anti-wall" strategy. Now, the State of

the Union is confirmed on the calendar. The
interesting parts won't be about the wall as much
as they will be about China.

China—the one thing that could unite all sides of
American debates. Beware the peace of a nation in
need of an enemy to unify them, for that peace may
be shortlived.

Hot on the Capitol Hill agenda is Obama's DACA
program (Deferred Action for Childhood Arrivals).
The argument basically goes that young trees can
be transplanted, but once they have grown, re-
transplanting them again can kill them. Children
are innocent and—though beneficiaries of the free
economy, free speech, and freedom of America's
wonderful and ought-to-be-sought socioeconomic
system—children would not be at-fault for receiving
the great benefit of America's growing greatness.
So, why punish the children? That's the argument
in DACA's defense.

One example that isn't used enough to defend
DACA is the Back-to-Africa movement, of the
1800s, which sought to return Black Americans to
Africa. The idea was absurd, demonstrating no
knowledge of international life and culture. Though
an injustice, forcing a reversal after history has
moved on only makes the injustice worse. DACA

was such an injustice and the way forward cannot be explained in, shall we say, "black and white".

From the Conservative perspective, the best solution to DACA claimants (the children in question) is to punish the perpetrators, not the children. In other words, punish the parents. The following course would do just that: Any illegally entered parents must report themselves and prepare for deportation or, with a clean criminal record, be given 30 days to prepare for a speedy and unconditional return to their home country. Then, children wishing to claim DACA status must meet minimum age and circumstantial requirements *that prove returning to a life in their family's country would cause a lower-quality life, such as not knowing the language or already having developed American credentials, must not have citizenship with that nation, and be banned from any dual citizenship with that nation for ten years.*

This would cut off the parents from their children. If they wanted their children to be American because of America's greatness, this would give them that at a price worth paying. For anyone who thinks the price is not worth paying, the DACA benefits would not be necessary. Let the people choose themselves and let America be a place of immigrants willing to pay the price of freedom that never comes free.

Cadence of Conflict: Asia, February 4

The PDT Symphony *Asian Mad Scientist Theorem*** is hard at work—that history unfolds as if a mythical mad scientist has finished societal experimentation on North Korea and has now decided to implement the same principles in China, this time with a seemingly faster canter toward communist calamity. Rather than nukes, China makes noises of sinking US aircraft carriers and invading Taiwan.

The theorem is not truth, but it helps to accurately anticipate how history will unfold, and anticipate it has. It foretold that the mythical "miracle of China" would be exposed for the myth it always was.

The so-called "China miracle" seduced too many. There was no miracle happening inside China. There was no invention, no innovation, no new ideas. Even China's socioeconomic framework was reverse-engineered from Russian Marxism. Now, government requires itself to be the head of even religion; an Atheist government wants to define the truth for a religion that believes in a God that the government does not. How can that not be a course for calamity?

China gained its money, not from its own human ingenuity—since the Confucian education culture purges all ingenuity inclinations. No, the money came from Americans who would drive half a dollar's distance in gasoline to save a nickel—thinking that this made sense. It didn't make sense, it didn't save cents, but it did make dollars for China. But, now, those dollars are all gone—the dollars China believed in, and the dollars that made Western saps believe in China. The "miracle" was never from China, but from the United States' innovative, free-thinking, God-fearing economy.

China continues to grab for power—not because it feels powerful. While its economy and international respect have taken a nosedive, China is all the more adamant about "reclaiming" what is China's ostensibly by rite. The looming invasion of Taiwan won't happen because China believes it is economically strong enough to win, but that reclaiming Taiwan would solve all other problems to make China economically strong again. China believes China is a poor nation only because it hasn't yet "retaken" more control of more lands, such as Taiwan—an island that the Communist Party never once controlled.

Even King Belshazzar feared the writing on the wall without understanding it. But, Western saps didn't fear the writing written in their own economic language. Now, three Canadians are shocked and caught off guard. They should have known better than to put themselves in such peril during our dangerous times. So should the coupon clippers in America's consumer base have known better. So should the American companies about to watch their investments get "appropriated" have known better.

And, China should have known such a trade war was coming. Lack of reciprocity started the Opium Wars. China should have researched America's history books for the phrase "Indian giver", which often described America's government much more than it described America's Natives. China should have known that American consumers would respond in wrath when their jobs had been exported from their homes and imported into a country that prohibits free speech and religion. China should have known that a trade war was in the making from the first day that American manufacturers outsourced their labor to the Chinese.

But, the Americans never told China because the Americans were too consumed with their own consumerism.

The obvious has been ignored. Now, the incvitable results are playing out. Whatever course history takes, the results must run their course, but we know it won't be pretty, not for a while anyway. But, of all the things it never was, it was always foreseeable to those who wanted to look at what was right in front of them.

It takes two to start a war, so everyone should have known the war that was starting because everyone was starting it long, long ago.

Encore of Revival: America, February 11

If the border wall dispute goes to a point of emergency, there would be implications. How deeply the administration and Congress will want to pursue those implications is a question to itself, with a likely answer of, "Not far." But, the implications will remain.

Declaring a national emergency at the border is basically a declaration of being invaded by a civilian army. Like any army, this army also has a purpose and a moral cause they think to be right and fair. What invading army doesn't? But, it would be an invading army of some kind or another because that's what Constitutional powers the president would need to use to declare the emergency: *repel against invasion.*

The Constitutional language here compels Congress to act. If Trump were to declare an emergency to deal with the border situation—then a Federal judge stopped him—that judge would be just as implicated as Congress.

The implication?—Conspiracy with the enemy.

If an invasion can be stopped, but won't be stopped by Congress or a judge, then they are conspirators with that invasion. This is because they are Constitutionally required to stop *any* force from invading, not only a deputized army sanctioned by a recognized state.

Trump might not be able to do much. Presidents can't impeach anyone and members of Congress don't answer for anything they do as elected officials to anyone except the electorate. He might be able to fire the Federal judge, but that won't achieve anything because another treacherous scoundrel is sure to pop up elsewhere.

But, the implication will be there. What to do about it will be left up to the voters.

Cadence of Conflict: Asia, February 11

Trump fell a few dots shy of declaring all out war against China in his State of the Union address. He spoke kindly of China, then brought back Cold War era talk of "defeating Communism". He also said he wanted China to have to play by the same rules as Russia and the US where nuclear missiles are concerned. The Chinese won't like that because they genuinely believe they are better than everyone else.

China's ancient, recently best-kept-secret, aspiration of saturating the world with the "Han" bloodline is in full swing. The recent spotlight has been the Han migration that threatens to dilute and eventually eliminate Uyghurs from the Xinjiang Uyghur "autonomous region" in China—one of many "provinces under protest" that reject forced assimilation into China's bossy political ideology—an ideology Trump threatened in announcing his goal that China come down to the lowly level of having to play by the same rules as everyone else.

Then, there was military defense. Trump's speech was patriotic. He celebrated "American exceptionalism" and the US's role in helping save people in other countries from tyranny. Some call it a "messiah complex". Some call it "American charity". Whatever it was, Trump stirred the hearts of Americans to remember their roots of militarily helping those in need, announcing massive military investment, and reviving America's old war on Communism.

The US is already preparing for war with China—in the old fashioned, soft, "humble" way, according to its Christendom roots of Chivalry. Without the pomp and parade, China's imperialistic culture may not even notice. But, war drums are sounding on the horizon. Trump's trade talks are either an irritant or a stall tactic—probably both.

Encore of Revival: America, February 18

The brewing fight between the president and Congress will only strengthen the executive office. Even if a toned-down compromise is reached after a Supreme Court review, whatever the president would get out of it would be more power than he had clarified to him without the lawsuit. In the future, if Anti-Trumpists were to riot again as they have elsewhere, Trump may be able to take executive action against the riots—but having cried, "Wolf!" one too many times, the Left might have no powers left to stop him.

Building the national emergency declaration from components used by Obama serves two purposes. Firstly, and more obviously, are the optics. By opposing Trump's declaration, opponents would be opposing Obama. But, that is mere optics, no matter how much hypocrisy it may demonstrate. Secondly, and far more importantly, court orders that restrict Trump's declaration would need to tread carefully in dissent because any dissent against Trump could be used as a precedent to reverse or even take settlement-seeking action against Obama's executive work in the past. Suing

Trump for this order could unwittingly become an attack against Obama from his own supporters.

Russianewsgategate is imploding quietly, as was entirely foreseeable—and social media giants along with it. With Google having shown Taiwanese military secrets to the world, heavy regulation could come faster than thought, but that's where matters in Asia and America meet in these Pacific times.

Cadence of Conflict:
Asia, February 18

Google's negligence with Taiwanese military secrets certainly put Taiwan on the map—and it may list Google among the utilities. Being made into a public utility by force is a mild settlement for de facto espionage.

Taiwanese military tech is also growing. At an expo in Abu Dhabi, Taiwan hopes to sell its own tech to the Middle East; including its own supersonic anti-ship missiles. If China's tech were so supreme, China would be courting the patronage of Middle Eastern states. Credibility is often in the money.

While trade talks drag on and on—and on and on—even the Leftist press supports President Trump in standing against China. Ah, yes—the one thing China hates about the West most of all: elections. Nothing could guarantee a sitting president's re-election like a war against the self-polluted giant who ate America's jobs. America's ping-pong game of "talk and smack" with China continues. Wait until the US cozies up to Taiwan even more—with the Google spill being a perfect excuse—after the Huawei CFO suspect gets extradited to the US.

Encore of Revival: America, February 25

This was a week of fakery and desperation. Pacific Daily Times did not pick up the Jussie story of the fake beating because, quite frankly, something about it just didn't seem newsworthy—until now. Initial headlines weren't clear as to what exactly happened, except that there was an actor doing something. It seemed reminiscent of—and turned out to actually be much like—Jordan Brown's story, the homosexual pastor from Texas who dropped his lawsuit about the word "fag" on his cake, after Whole Foods—the bakery—filed a countersuit that he had tampered with the cake. Jussie Smollett was by no means the first, but the fake media just didn't know how to see a fake for a fake. Perhaps that's because they'd have to implicate themselves—perhaps.

Pro-Abortion movements are getting laws passed in Democratic-leaning States. This anticipates a likely national ban of abortion from the Supreme Court. Effort itself is not progress. Interpret the times correctly; this effort indicates progress already made on behalf of the Pro-Life movement.

Just the same, Mueller's coming report is something the Democrats should want to keep quiet, not only because it will acquit Donald Trump of conspiracy with Russia, but because it will likely reveal a breadcrumb trail leading to dirt on the Democrats. With the report not yet delivered, this can't be certain, but it is how history tends to work. The false accuser's accusations often turn against him.

Cadence of Conflict: Asia, February 25

Nations and peoples of the free world are reaching toward each other. The EU reached out to Taiwan and Taiwan was grateful. Taiwan reached out to CNN and CNN did an interview. Kim Jong Un is likely on a train headed through China to Vietnam to meet President Trump. President Trump met with the Vice Premier of China in the Oval Office to discuss trade. And, China "rightly" oppresses an estimated two million Muslims in internment camps, who inhabit the hope-to-breakaway province of Xinjiang, through which China's "Silk Road" passes to reach other nations with trillions of dollars in trade.

Taiwan's position in the world only stepped up. In tech, it's the multinational victim of China. The EU's unanimous statement of support for Taiwan and condemnation of China's military activity in the Taiwan Strait is anything but positive PR for China. Taiwan has the support of Europe; that doesn't count for nothing.

China's latest shenanigans include Hong Kong taking a serious look at redefining extradition laws so that Taiwanese in Hong Kong would be "extradited" to China. This does far more damage for Hong Kong's popularity with its electorate at home than it does for Taiwan, raising international sympathy for both. Remember, meddling in Hong Kong's government is a "must not" as the condition of Hong Kong not remaining under Britain. Nothing would indicate Chinese meddling in Hong Kong's government more than such a sure-to-backfire anti-PR move like Hong Kong is making by even entertaining such a revision.

The fingerprints of Beijing damaging Hong Kong where British interests remain, all in order to damage Taiwan, goes against the wisdom of courting favor with the masses across Europe. Then, there's Huawei.

As if international scandals implicating China weren't enough, Huawei's founder made the narcissistic comment that "the world can't live without Huawei". In Chinese culture, that might make enough people feel compelled to comply. But, the God-fearing West will take the self-absorbed claim as a challenge, much how God took the challenge when "experts" said He couldn't sink the Titanic. Huawei just might take its place in the hall of sunken fame. No, the West does not. Not too many years from now, when a finance guru claims that a company is "too big to fall", the public will respond, "Remember Huawei."

Encore of Revival: America, March 4

The conclusion of the current media analysis of Trump is clear: the Democrats and media sing in unison. Their song is one of contradiction—that Obama's routine use of executive authority and the Clinton's scandals should have been ignored—but not Trump, who uses executive authority to obey the Constitution to defend the nation's borders when Congress will not. His dedication to obey the Constitution is his crime, the lesser-than Obama-Clinton scandals are just the means of punishing him for doing what is right.

At a time when America's enemies make threats, the people have a president who won't play the "surrender" role expected by the "great surrenderers" of society. The Russianewsgategate fiasco is about to hit the fan and spray mud all over the Left. Media criticism of the president's speech at CPAC makes no sense. He celebrates heroes, explains the inside baseball of trade, listens to the wisdom of our military's generals, and gave the microphone to a young man who was punched in the face for his beliefs. The news media

is being seen more and more for the villain it is—
and the people know all about it.

41

Cadence of Conflict: Asia, March 4

Buffoons became naysayers this week, arguing that tit-for-tat military drill concessions would be the path to peace and that progress without finality in Hanoi surmounted to failure.

Trump knows exactly what he is doing. Progress without "too much too fast", passing up the invitation to stop in China while visiting Kim Jong-Un in Vietnam, replacing large military drills with detailed tactical exercises in South Korea, standing with the Philippines against "an armed attack" from China in the South Sea, delaying a tariff hike with China while inviting Xi to Mar-a-Lago, scrutinizing Chinese-funded "learning centers" in America—it all plays right into a larger overall strategy of strength and resolve in Asia.

As the US and China inch toward a trade agreement, Taiwan makes larger and larger strides asserting its independent activity. Backed by a recent US court ruling, Taiwan's presence will only irritate China. Trade talk is part of the precarious path ahead. No trade agreement is enough to mitigate other disagreements between the US and

China. The only way would require the US to surrender, and that's not about to happen.

43

Encore of Revival: America, March 11

The nation is polarizing. Conservatives are becoming more conservative; Liberals are becoming more liberal. The veil of mediocrity has been lifted and people are being forced to fly their true colors.

Democratic Congresswoman Omar from Minnesota called out Obama for being a "pretty face" more "polished" than Trump, while denouncing Obama's policies. Freshman Congresswoman Cortez and veteran Senator Sanders decried capitalism while unemployment is at a record low and jobs are returning to America—jobs which Obama said would not come back. That only adds to the lists of failed Obama promises. Yet, Democrats still think it was the Obama ideological opposition that failed, not their own—except for Omar who thinks everyone failed, kind of.

It's one thing to not know when one lost, it's another thing to not know when one will lose again. What better place to discuss a campaign for the anti-enterprise 2020 ticket than in the Caribbean!

Socialist cities across America are in a battle against rural American sheriffs and prosecutors.

Don't attack people with your posts on social media—but if you're CNN, that's common practice, though still defamation—at least according to the lawyer for the Covington High School student who was treated by CNN and the Washington Post the way Facebook doesn't want you to treat real bad guys who actually did something wrong—maybe. It all depends on opinion, but there is one solution: utilities.

Facebook and Google are in the fast lane on the highway to "Utilityhood". Irritating as it is, a free market can't force Facebook to cooperate with Vine when there is neither profit nor loss in our "free-and-open" Internet. By allowing Facebook to make market decisions in its own interests, it will be easier to sway public opinion toward government crushing the Facebook and Google empires by making them public utilities.

Cadence of Conflict: Asia, March 11

China doesn't get the message, likely because China is too self-absorbed in its own culture. Detaining Canadians will provoke Canadians to support action against China to have the detained Canadians released—even supporting military action. When the US and China finally officiate their conflict, Canada may join the fray, all thanks to Beijing belligerence.

The Western press inches up its hardline against China every day. Even Europe reports on social media censorship in China. This comes on the 60th anniversary of the Tibetan Uprising. China closed visits to Tibet for this reason. But, that doesn't matter since Taiwan could see a visit from the US Secretary of Health and Human Services as well as the Dalai Lama.

Speaking of Taiwan, the self-ruled island is arming to the teeth. They just put in a request with the US, asking whatever military equipment they should buy so their military will be stronger than China's.

Northern Korea has all the indications of someone whispering in their ears, encouraging and emboldening against peace with the US. After Trump met with Kim, after he returned home to the States to find a message that Kim would be less cooperative, Kim had spent significant time in China. Now, we have more indications that North Korea is continuing missile tests. The bigger problem in Korean North is that the people know the Hanoi Summit did not get economic sanctions lifted—Northern Koreans are learning the truth, despite controls on speech and information.

Now, Pakistan has put China in a precarious spot. The recent "explosive" squabble between Pakistan and India attracted Western eyes. It's great that Pakistan wants to go after terror cells within its borders, but it's terrible that Pakistan doesn't go after terror cells that launch attacks against India. Pakistan buys weapons from both the US and China. The US won't sell fighter jets to Pakistan for use against India; China would—or would it? If China did, then China would be backing the backing of terrorism. So, little, tiny Pakistan has tipped the balance against China by being friendly with China as a weapons buyer.

So, all Chinese eyes are on Pakistan—and India and North Korea and Taiwan.

Encore of Revival: America, March 18

The twelve Senators who voted to continue the mess at the border included the soon-to-be notorious "three amigos"—Paul, Romney, and Rubio. The other Senator from Utah, Mike Lee, also voted with Mitt. Of the other eight, two are up for re-election in 2020—Lamar Alexander of Tennessee and Susan Collins of Maine. It will be interesting to see if they get re-elected.

Opposition to Trump only makes him stronger— and the office of the president along with him. Once again, it seems Democrats and "never-Trump" Republicans, like the three amigos, are part of some conspiracy too obvious to recognize. Even the Mueller fiasco helps Trump amass his army of voters.

Congressional Democrats want to make the Mueller situation partially public by making Mueller's report public—while keeping silent the dark beginnings of the "Russianewsgategate" scandal that started it all. Mueller's so-called "investigation" is more akin to something between a chicken randomly running circles with its head cut off and a headless horseman—maybe more of a headless horseman riding a headless chicken. The so-called "investigation's" new nickname could be "the headless chickenman."

Senator Lindsey "Grahamnesty" sure is coming out of his shell! He was formerly known as the senator who got along. But, ever since the Kavanaugh witch trial in the Senate, something in Senator Graham seems to have snapped—and it isn't unsnapping. He was most outspoken in blocking the biased release of Mueller's "headless chickenman" report.

Now, the State of Washington thinks that a State can over-ride the Constitutional requirements for Federal elections. Here we go...

Cadence of Conflict: Asia, March 18

Drama and theatrics! The US might be in a position to enforce the Magnitsky Act against China. Now, like Taiwan before, the US is taking the pot shots. It compares to Tony Stark's *Iron Man* tossing rocks at a tank to provoke the tank before obliterating the tank.

Talk of talks about trade with China while focusing on more military money for what Acting Defense Secretary Patrick Shanahan calls "China, China, China"—that's not an effort to make peace with a country that wants it, but an effort to irritate a not-so-closet adversary into justifying a retaliatory victory. China will see the US as two-faced, never figuring out that the US is intentionally getting under Beijing's skin because the Chinese don't know how easily irritable their view of themselves makes them.

Then, there's Korea. In a retelling from *The Godfather III*, we might say that Kim wouldn't do this without backing. By rumbling about nuking up again, Kim is flexing muscles that shouldn't be flexed—but only would be flexed if someone, say like Xi Jinping, were whispering support in his ear.

More is going on than even Trump may be revealing, even if Kim's rumblings are all for show. If tensions rise between the US and Northern Korea, China would be the likely backstage culprit. That would mean that tension in the Koreas would justify US action against China—yet another tank rock to toss.

Then, we have "melo-theatrics" worse than "damn lies": statistics.

If Trump's poll numbers were to suddenly plummet, nothing would bring them back like a victory against evermore unpopular China—now at 41% in America. That makes Trump, 47% as of Tuesday, more popular than China. If House Democrats were to take action against Trump, that might encourage China that he would not be able to sustain action against China—when actually a victorious action against China would bring up his popularity to make him politically immune to House Democrats. The freedom and opinion - driven dynamics of American politics eludes Chinese strategists, another front on which Beijing is likely to miscalculate.

If Trump's popularity were to slip just before a conflict with China, it could have been intentional —as a means to provoke China into thinking that China is stronger against the US than it is. But,

China will never figure it out, like the cat chasing
the laser pen's dot—they never figure it out.

52

Encore of Revival: America, March 25

American immigrants fleeing communism are tending to lean right, according to reports. Memories of the dark regimes they escape come flooding back as they watch Democratic talking points. This wasn't how the Democratic minds planned things to play out.

But, that's how things play out in a witch hunt. A concluded investigation with no indictment is, by definition, an exoneration. While an opinion may certainly, surely have "middle ground", prosecution does not—a person is either prosecuted or not prosecuted. Trump is not being prosecuted. Being "not exonerated" is a matter of opinion. Mueller does not write the opinion of the voters anymore than the voters write the report for Mueller.

If Democrats push the Mueller report as a basis to prosecute or even impeach Trump, then they set a precedent to prosecute Hillary. The Democrats lost, if nothing else roughly $20 million dollars (directly and indirectly reported) over two years, but neither indited Trump nor does it look like they will be able to impeach him, given public opinion. Politically, the non-indictment has already exonerated him, regardless of the non-indicting report's opinion to the contrary.

Rod Rosenstein's slow exit can easily be explained by his new boss. Since William Barr took over the absent Attorney General's desk just one moth ago, he needed a veteran so he could catch up to speed. The concern that Rosenstein stayed in office too long after he was supposed to leave could also be applied to the Mueller investigation that should have been over much more quickly. Two endless endings that lack direction should be expected to end together.

The Federal Reserve needs reforming. According to Jerome Powell, the Fed chairman who holds a position appointed by the president, the president had no impact on the Fed's recent decisions. Especially with so much talk of "accountability" orbiting squanderous theatrics like in the Mueller solar system, entities that lack accountability need it.

Cadence of Conflict: Asia, March 25

Now, China has become the dark example of why not to be a Democrat in America. This is a new low. As much as being compared to China makes Democrats appear bad, it makes China appear all the worse because it paints China as the archetype of "how not to be". American sentiment against China grows evermore glum.

No country is above democratic politics. Though Communist, China is still controlled by democracy. If the American public doesn't like China, they will overthrow China in their own way. But, that's a concept Beijing is incapable of adapting to because they have no such accountability to their own people at home.

China thinks its "rise to power" is about China being able to make decisions on its own. America thinks that anyone's rise to power is about growing up and acting like an adult. As long as China keeps saying things like, "China can do what we want, America can't tell us what to do," it keeps getting evermore clear whether China is an adult yet.

Taiwan isn't backing down. The government there continues to press for WHO participation. A Taiwanese airline now has flights to the island of Palau—which is important because it is a good thing that didn't happen under Beijing control. A Taiwanese Mayor of Kaohsiung, Han, of the pro-unification-leaning political KMT-Nationalist party visited the Beijing office in Hong Kong—raising questions about honesty and motive in Taiwan's central government.

His party keeps threatening to make laws to help Taiwan be re-unified under Beijing. That party recently won a mid-term at local governments. Perhaps they want to loose the next national election just as quickly.

Now, the US is in serious talks about establishing a strong military presence on Taiwan's Taiping Island, somewhere between Taiwan's huge, main island and China's man-made islets at Mischief Reef. That would lead to a provocation that no trade agreement could withstand.

Encore of Revival: America, April 1

The message from the EU is clear: "Join us so if you leave we can make you suffer for it." Now, Italy cozies up to China?

Boeing tried to mount too big an engine on too small a plane because the engine used less fuel. This changed the plane's aerodynamic personality; software was their solution. But, with software come bugs. So, Boeing had a warning light option if the software got too buggy. Ethiopian and Lion Air chose not to spend the $80k extra for the warning light. That cost Boeing about $40B in stock value. Now, we see that the FAA had turned a half-blind eye.

But, many other warnings have been ignored. America is polarizing. The only things deeper than the deep pockets of the US Treasury are the Left's demands for spending. Senate Democrats silently watched the "Green New Deal" go down in flames. Cities may follow. When the going gets tough, the Right gets working while the Left gets burning hot mad.

Immigration is broken, not just in America, but everywhere. We need a proper on-ramp for good foreigners to enter any country. But, vitriol doesn't make reforms. There is a difference between vitriol and a "tantrump". Trump has achieved far more in two years than Obama did in eight. Still the Left stays vitriolic. That's their only strategy, it seems.

The Left doesn't want the Right to survive. The Right wants everyone to have the room to work and thrive. Neither will back down.

*Peggy Noonan wrote in the Wall Street Journal:**

[quote]

Yes, America is polarizing more than ever before. Who wins? We'll see.

The Two Americas Have Grown Much Fiercer, March 28, 2019

Cadence of Conflict: Asia, April 1

China is being overwhelmed—Huawei to the west, British probes to the south, Kim to the north, but the prospect of trade to the east. The weakness is in the Chinese-cultural paradigm of negotiation. Chinese culture wants to sign a contract first, then negotiate the terms after. That's a polite way of explaining "psychopathic negotiation".

China labels Hong Kong as an "internal", national security matter. It's not; it's a "joint" matter. According to the 1984 Sino-British Joint Declaration, China can't govern Hong Kong as its own until 2047—a mandate for Hong Kong being under Beijing's leadership. By telling Britain to "face reality", London will see the reality as Beijing reneging on the deal. It's not that China wants to be malicious, but that China doesn't understand what a promise really entails.

That could be why the Chinese offer such sweeping concessions to get better trade with America. They might not understand that promises about those concessions will actually have to be kept. But, there's more that sails over Beijing's brightest heads.

America shows no indication of backing down on Taiwan. By cozying up on trade, Beijing probably hopes America will receive an indirect message about Taiwan. But, if Taiwan isn't discussed, then it's not part of the trade agreement—or any agreement with the US. Beijing, probably laden with more wishful thinking than savvy, won't understand. They just won't understand.

That's the Korean problem to the north. Trump knew exactly what he was doing by telling Kim exactly what "de-nuking" looked like. They had talked before. Kim had taken a three day journey to talk again. Now Kim knows reality: a free economy prospers, North with nukes has neither in the end. That won't go over well with a culture more prideful than the Chinese. Trump knows this.

Now, Kim is a loose canon to China's north and the only thing Trump did was unleash the obvious. We'll see how long it takes for China to understand, if ever.

Encore of Revival: America, April 8

America is on the quiet this week. It's the deep calm before the storm. People are tired. Unsatisfied opponents of Conservatism are getting wary from victory deferred after victory deferred. Now, they are looking to another failed candidate to put their hope in, Sanders.

Insanity is doing the same thing over and over, expecting different results. The invented Mueller Russianewsgategate scandal scandal is coming to its grand fizzle-and-pop of an ending. The Left is self-destructing with its old playbook tactic. When melodrama isn't enough to get what they want, they respond with more melodrama.

Kirstjen Nielsen is finally gone. Since the "New York Times Essay", the public grew suspicious of insiders trying to sabotage the Trump administration. In the Pacific Daily Times Symphony list of suspects, she was right there at the top with John Kelly. (See Encore articles from September 10, November 19, and December 10 of 2018.) Firing both discretely and far apart was among the best ways to handle saboteurs. Were they? Only Trump knows for sure, and that's the way it should stay.

Cadence of Conflict: Asia, April 8

America's government has finally cracked the code on China. They know how to get under China's skin. They had an idea before, but the algorithm—the precise frequency of activation—needed fine-tuning. And, of course, China made it all too easy to know that the code had been cracked. The sale of 60 F-16V's to Taiwan—inferior in both number and, supposedly, technology—wasn't even made official. Still, China couldn't wait to announce to the world exactly the kind of insignificance that it found irritating above all previous attempts.

With this new and tested knowledge, we can expect the US to do more, and to do so more subtly. America will stand calmly, smiling. China will fume more every day, seemingly for no reason. At last, the Chinese will be so overwhelmed with rage that they will strike before military wisdom advises.

The sad, but poetic, part is that no warnings, not even reading this article, not even a spy exposing some kind of "provocation plot" or whatnot would be able to deter China from this fate. For, China loves respect above all else. Those who hunger for respect are easy to provoke and anyone provoked is under complete control of the provocateur. And, Chinese culture doesn't know how to change or even listen.

But, there is another factor that blinded China to the American tactics. A nation with a one-child policy won't have as much experience in sibling rivalry. America doesn't have such a policy. Americans learn from childhood how to get under some else's skin—especially when that someone else is the known playground bully who needs to be provoked to a brawl and sent to the principle's office before getting any older, and bigger.

The die has been cast. The fate of the American-Chinese war has already been determined: China strikes; China loses; China loses more. Now, it's just a matter of watching how the specifics play out on our road to the foreseen.

Encore of Revival: America, April 15, 2018

With the last of Symphony's saboteur suspects being expelled from the Trump administration, establishment Republicans have their undies in a bunch. Their objections indicate two main motives. Toward the surface, they still think Trump's decisions are based on calculation of "election strategery" rather than made by an administrator who wants certain things done a certain way. But, on a deeper level, they don't want their stable, "established" world being unraveled by anyone, outsider or not. But then, there is a third, less apparent layer, more sinister—a question of whether they knew about the saboteurs and wanted them to stay there. Publicized opposition to the president of their own party certainly proves the kind of character that would undermine their own party's president by any means.

Now that Russianewsgategate nonsense is being seen for the yesterday's yesterday's tabloid newspaper it always was, the media machine is gearing up to save face: Goldman Sachs thinks Trump might be re-electable. The Left doesn't get it. The most important two things to understand about Donald Trump is that from the time he announced his candidacy, 1. he was always going to be elected and 2. he was always going to be re-elected. Those two things aren't obvious to people who don't understand Donald Trump.

Democratically-controlled "sanctuary cities" have been working, as they purport, to be a safe haven for immigrants. The kinds of immigrants they seek to protect, as they purport, will be helpful to their communities and to the nation. Now, they have a splendid and long-hoped-for hope of seeing their hard efforts pay off. They will be the beneficiaries of thousands of exactly the kinds of, as they purport, good people they have been standing up to defend. Yet, they found a way to be angry.

If the Trump administration were to send immigrants to the very cities hoping to be sanctuaries for them, wouldn't that be a good thing? One would think so, unless sanctuary city laws were known to be designed to create problems. By objecting to getting what they wanted, Democrats imply that they know something that they purport everyone else doesn't. Is there something wrong about sanctuary city laws that their Democratic leaders aren't telling us?

The rest of America—the "fly-over" counties, the rural areas that the Democratic cosmopolitans turn their noses up at, the Conservatives who grow everyone's food and cling to their "guns and religion"—they were suspicious about sanctuary city laws. They thought it might be a bad idea. If the Conservatives were right, then sending the invited immigrants to the party that invited them could create a breakdown of law, paving the way for the Federal Government to declare martial law and deal with sanctuary city policy makers that way.

Just imagine: Trump-controlled Democratic cities —and it all would have been made possible by Democrats. But, that's assuming that the Conservatives were right. We'll see.

Cadence of Conflict: Asia, April 15

Events in China are playing out according to the "Pacific Daily Times Symphony *Asian Mad Scientist Theorem*"**. The experimental phase in North Korea is finished and methods are being applied throughout China on a much grander scale. This week, we see reports of expensive ghost cities, comparable to Pyongyang. The debt to build those ghost cities could be enough to break China's economy into the deprived status of northern Korea. Now, swelling human rights concern could court the West to support China's unfriendly neighbors to intervene in China as the "grand liberators".

If things continue on track with the theorem, China would end up in an armistice against its own provinces—a standoff between Beijing and fragments of the soon-to-be-formerly united China.

Trump continues to prove that he knows what he's doing with Kim Jong-Un. The DPRK's Great Successor will likely wise up, still venting steam once in a while. He seems to be one of the smartest heads of state in his region—seeking more cooperation with economic policies that work, not less. But even if not, Korea will not be a border for China to ignore. Beijing and its surrounding provinces would be the likely hold-out against a liberated Northwest, Tibet, Southern Canton, and it will need to keep a 24/7 guard in the Northeast. Break-aways could form their own federation, or not. Either way, as history repeats, we look to be headed for a Cold War -style standoff between fractured Chinese regions.

The US Marines are test driving "lightning carriers"—small aircraft carriers with a potently packed punch of F-35s. Their range radius is smaller, but so is their targetable shadow. In a Pacific conflict, a smattering of lightning carriers might prove more formidable than a single, central Nimitz class group. Federated, autonomous, small attack groups tend to be wise in warfare, as the French Revolution proved on land. We'll see at sea.

These smaller carriers are said to focus on smaller tasks, putting Nimitz class carriers—now being called "super carriers"—in the spotlight against China and Russia. And, we know that the Chinese think the spotlight is an indication of "importance". While Russia knows better, the Chinese probably don't. Just because headlines read that a Nimitz class focuses on China doesn't mean US strategy would fail if China's new "anti-carrier" missiles sunk a Nimitz. Sinking a Nimitz class carrier would only enrage the American public into a war that they couldn't lose. That's how history has always played out, anyway. But, the mistakes from history don't seem to have much impact on Chinese President Xi, who is determined to revive Maoism at any cost. If Maoism is revived, it's results will follow. That won't end the standoff with Taiwan; it will add more uncontrolled lands to the standoff it was never strong enough to resolve.

Encore of Revival: America, April 22

Thinking about the Russianewsgategate scandal like an addictive drug explains everything. It provides a kind of fix to both sides of divided America. Mueller's report is the latest dose.

To the Right, it proves how fraudulent and one-sided the attacks on Trump were because there has been more justification for the near identical investigations into the Clintons since the 1990s. That energizes the Right to talk, persuade friends, and vote for Trump. And, the fact that Mueller failed to provide an indictment will draw some voters from the Left to the Right. To the persistent Left, the report contains enough "hopes of Easter eggs" that they can wake up yet another day thinking "this will be the day" when someone finds the "silver bullet" to get Trump impeached. And, of course, every Leftist reporter thinks, "I'll be the one to find and break the story."

The whole Mueller investigation, even the report, indicates that there never was any intention to act against Trump—not from Mueller, anyway. Rather, the purpose from the beginning was to toss doggy treats to both packs of the feuding dog pound.

Even some fringe politicians will clean up the scraps by running this election. Failing in one election after another can be a well-paying job, if one loses with valor. When the voters get depressed, they always have a dose of Mueller to give them enough of a high to keep them amused and tranquilized while not a single thing changes in Washington.

Tiger Woods made a dramatic comeback that will give inspiration and hope to many people around the world. Life isn't perfect nor are the people who live it. But, that doesn't mean we should give up. Happy Easter!

Cadence of Conflict: Asia, April 22

China faces more scrutiny from its own propaganda while Taiwan searches its own soul. Taiwanese elections are fast approaching. Demagoguery is in full swing. Even the founder of Foxconn says a Chinese god told him to run for president.

We could say that billionaires are the presidential trend, but Terry Gou's (郭台銘) money is largely in China, which is planning to attack Taiwan. Trump's investments were mainly in American companies with satellite projects globally. Gou can't rightly be compared to Trump. While there were proven-to-be-unsubstantiated suspicions of a connection to Russia with Trump, Gou's connection to China is both widely known and undisputed, Foxconn having 12 factories in China*. Gou opposes the US selling weapons to Taiwan. I wonder why.

If business tycoon Gou were to take the de facto pro-unification KMT-Nationalist party nomination, he would need to overcome Mayor Han of Kaohsiung, a populist with little political experience who's primary vehicle of campaigning is complaint and demagoguery. Han recently accused Taiwan's military of being "eunuchs" in uniform, which stirred up the voters who don't like compulsory military service, but he failed to provide a solid path to making any improvements.

The controlling party's incumbent president will need to face a primary challenger, former Premier and Mayor William Lai, who has his own past list of non-accomplishments.

While Taiwan fights with itself, China's new best-friend-forever is Venesuala. The press highlighted China's high-pressure work culture this week with a story about Alibaba founder Jack Ma's defense of 12-hour, 6-day work weeks. Did Ma think that would make the American public more or less likely to support US military action against China? Some in China are starting to see Trump as China's savior.

So, with a seemingly unstable Taiwan and a China with something to prove, we are approaching flashpoint, where "liberators" will get the justification they need to come out of the woodwork and split up China like fire ants on a dead tiger.

*https://en.wikipedia.org/wiki/Foxconn#China

Encore of Revival: America, May 6

While war brews in the Far East, the West debates social media. Populism is taking over from all sides. Even Conservatives aren't being so conservative in their rhetoric, though they still express their ideals at the election polls more than anywhere else. Liberals express their ideals everywhere they can.

Nancy Pelosi already has her strategy lined up no matter the outcome of the 2016 election. "Social justice warriors" are taking over the Left to such a point that Democrats as we know them may not be a viable party much longer. The institution will survive a bit longer, but it will change. Rosie O'Donnell and Megyn Kelly learned that the hard way; Joe Biden is about to.

Most debates are no longer two-sided. More and more issues themselves belong to either the Right or the Left. Conservatives don't want to hear about the Mueller investigation at all. Liberals don't want to hear reports on the economy. The only thing Congress and the country seem to be united on is China and support for Taiwan. For now, Americans

aren't finding many other reasons for unity at
home—for now.

Cadence of Conflict: Asia, May 6

Fibers are starting to snap and the solutions brought by governments always include adding more tension to the frayed rope.

China heads more toward Maoism. A nation headed at warp speed into its past already has its future known.

Taiwan wrestles with itself, seeking endorsement and recognition from other nations while chaotic governance at home makes its next election uncertain. But, two things grow stronger every day in Taiwan: military and resolve. That's a problem for some countries, one in particular.

If Taiwan isn't the last straw, Korea could be. North Korea launched a missile for the first time in a long time. That wouldn't have happened without backing.

The de facto consensus among the US, China, and everyone caught in between is simple: Make the rope snap ASAP by piling on as much load as possible. Even the strategy to improve Lockheed Martin's F-35 program comes in the form of complaint. The F-35s are ready to go. A dance floor

will magically appear in the Pacific once
Washington finishes playing with the bubble wrap.

Encore of Revival: America, May 13

War! That's next. With 2019 oaths of office sworn, with the 2020 presidential on the horizon, and with the Democrats clinging to demagoguery long after their fake investigation proved fake, the Left has left no alternative. War is one of the best ways to seal up a second term. Because it involves democracy, that is a calculation our Communist enemies can't understand. If the Communist world wanted to defeat the US—and if the communists in the Democratic Party wanted to defeat the Republicans—they'd play "peace possum" for two years. But, Communists have the learning curve of a cat.

The US is not moving resources to the Fifth Fleet in the Middle East because of some recent Iranian rhetoric. Iran makes and poses threats more often than North Korea. If Iran's most recent threats are special, it's from the smell of blood on the horizon as the sun comes up over the South Sea. Whether for caution or concern, the Pentagon is beefing-up the Fifth Fleet because the Seventh Fleet is about to get busy with China.

We don't want anyone taking advantage of the situation.

With Trump having pulled out of Syria and Afghanistan, Russia has every reason to be nice, for now. Extra missiles might make sure Iran does too—or if Iran can't get smart, at least change Iran along with the change about to happen to China. Moscow may tell Tehran to behave. New Delhi may feel emboldened give the same advice to Beijing, but you know cats.

War is coming and victory with it, both for the US and for the Republicans.

Cadence of Conflict: Asia, May 13

Trump knew the Chinese all along, all too well. The "trade war" never risked creating a real war; the "trade war" was a ploy the whole time—part of an elaborate scheme to provoke the Chinese into striking too soon. He says talks are going well with China—he can't not say that. China is indeed willing to have another talk. Trump announced tariff hikes and they still showed up. That's not exactly bad on the part of the Chinese.

Trade might never go well, but the talks certainly are for now. When has talk in politics ever looked bad?

But, don't make the mistake of thinking for even one second that negotiations aren't going exactly as Washington planned, whether with China or North Korea. The US provoked Japan through trade wars and embargoes leading up to WWII. This isn't just a strategy, it's a proven playbook tactic, and China's irritability is performing right on cue.

As Symphony said previously, the war will start when the US is ready to field-test the F-35 in an actual combat situation that we really need to win.

The F-35 was made for this and, like nuclear technology at the end of WWII, if the US doesn't use its fifth-generation fighter jets before Russia and China perfect theirs, it will have failed its initial purpose. Japan is ready to buy the worlds largest non-US fifth-generation F-35 fleet. They want the Marines' vertical take-off model for their helicopter carriers. Perhaps those carriers also had a purpose all along.

Talk isn't deteriorating, not with China anyway, but trade suddenly is. That's because the F-35 is ready to make its entrance onto the world's stage. Taiwan's election could prove to be a convenient lynch pin.

Businessmen are the presidential trend. Foxconn Chair and Founder Terry Gou is running under the KMT, a political party whose platform is "Chinese-Taiwan re-unification", yet he demands that China recognize Taiwan's history of de facto existence; China never will. Moving some production from among Foxconn's twelve factories in China back to Taiwan in Kaohsiung shows that his loyalties don't reside in Beijing nor in Nanjing as KMT old-hats still pine for. He's also beefing up supply in Houston, Indianapolis, and Mexico, atop his newest plant in Wisconsin. That will make the US less dependent on China and better ready for war. As an accomplished businessman, Terry will tear up the inexperienced populist Mayor Han of Kaohsiung in the primaries. After all, he brought jobs back to Kaohsiung.

Even if Gou loses primary or presidency, his campaign rhetoric, though less unacceptable to China than others, could force all other viable candidates to sympathize with Taiwan independence, if that proves to be the only electable platform. That's more than likely. Equally likely, China will see no way to "talk" its way toward absorbing Taiwan. Talk would thus breakdown and "the military option" would be the trigger in the gas tank known as the South Sea. Then, F-35 moves to centerstage.

Trump says China has one month. If we make it that long, then China would be stupider than we thought because the F-35s would have more time to fuel up.

Encore of Revival: America, May 20

The Supreme Court always sides with the courts retaining their power. Justice Kavanaugh's recent ruling with the Liberal side of the court was not any attempt to appeal to the Left. It demonstrates his knowledge of the tech world of developers and his belief that judges should be able to judge. The remaining Conservative justices on the Court sided with precedent, not with business reality. The Liberals on the Court simply ruled against business and monopoly with their activist ideals. Kavanaugh was the only justice who ruled objectively, notwithstanding that courts always rule in favor of the courts retaining their power to rule.

The Mueller investigation certainly served its double purpose. Communists in both the Democratic base and in the Chinese government held on to a delusional hope that Trump was weak. That kept them distracted and foolish long enough for them to ensnare themselves. China overreached, providing a great "election enemy", and the Leftist machine overreached, possibly incriminating themselves.

Some states turned Democratic in the recent midterm. But, things look like they're turning around for a gargantuan victory for Republicans nation-wide. Republican states are passing anti-abortion legislation that could lead to the long-waited reversal of Roe v Wade.

Cadence of Conflict: Asia, May 20

Of course China wanted to "re-negotiate". Chinese culture, whether in government or business, seeks to sign a contract first, then negotiate the terms after. In America it's called "reneging". In China is called "that strange, silly, sign a contract game the Americans require that makes no sense". Trump has known that since he had his ties made in China, maybe earlier.

Now, the American provocation machine is in full-swing. An executive order banning Huawei and a DOJ prosecution of Chinese hackers—all while planning another meeting in Japan next month—this isn't failed diplomacy. In the past month, China lobbed one too many objections to US action, thus providing the telemetry the US needed for the final calibrations on the Chinese irritation machine. That machine is up and running and won't stop. It will keep producing irritation at the speed of a 5G network.

As said last week, the problem of the F-35 was already known because the US was no longer interested in searching. This week, we found out

the specifics: a fuel tube. Now, we just need to wait
for distribution and replacement to get set up.

87

Encore of Revival: America, May 27

The dark forces that have commandeered the party Andrew Jackson started are on full display. Investigation findings are being released that will purportedly prove use of politically-neutral government institutions to investigate political opponents.

In terms of pre-election analysis, Republicans win by energizing the base. Nothing will energize the Republican base like the declassification about to drop onto the other end of what Mueller was investigating, except one thing. War with China is coming.

Censorship is having a blossom effect and it is difficult to know how it will end, other than to know that public utility status is coming for any company deemed to be a social media giant. Radicals don't exist on any single end of political spectrums. When one radical end calls for censorship of the entire half of the other spectrum, boomerang and escalation effects soon kick in. But, the call for censorship from the ever self-radicalizing Left was so extreme in degree and scope, it made a monster that couldn't not grow beyond the control of its mad creator. Now, it isn't as predictable as a boomerang nor does it escalate in nice, even, measured steps.

The wars of China and Mueller are much easier to predict than the zombie war created by censorship.

Cadence of Conflict: Asia, May 27

President Trump's response to Kim Jong-Un's recent missile party neither shows lack of a plan nor lack of respect for Japan; it show patience and insight. Gaining and maintaining trust and respect in difficult situations requires sureness in action and slowness in harsh words. Talk is cheap. These are politics, after all.

Trump has taken no action nor signed any orders giving Kim more permission. Many pundits and opinion commentators have speculated that Trump will have difficulty with Abe because of his patient words for Kim, but all of this speculation is speculation only. They are presenting a model to analyze Trump's decisions, but that model is devoid of a grid of *using "kind words" in the face of betrayal.* Kim's strategy has not deviated: provoke a US response. Trump's words "defuse" that strategy, so to speak. Trump is no pretentious fool, more of a patient father.

The situation in China, however is heating up, obviously for the same reasons. Trump and Xi exchange similar words as Trump gives in response to Kim's actions. They promise to prepare for talks while rallying their own citizens against each other. Rumors of peace are the surest sign that there is none just as provocation indicates a peace not easily broken.

Taiwan is gearing up for war, its war machine in full motion. Taiwan is beginning mass production of strategic strike responses. Taiwan is renaming one of its offices to include both "US" and "Taiwan" in the name, which is a first. These are not actions that have any intention of appeasing Beijing.

Then, there's Hong Kong. Responses from the American government would view the SAR as no longer capable of diplomatic ties if the extradition law on the table is passed. This extradition law would likely isolate Hong Kong from North America and Europe. We know war is close, but "how close" will be known by whether Beijing allows "Asia's World City" to internationally isolate itself.

Those promised and prepared talks between Beijing and Washington will only serve as size-ups, if they even happen.

Encore of Revival: America, June 3

America is dividing between the "hopers" and the "doers". On the one hand, many voters look for hope through our current times. On the other hand, voters work hard and smart to push the times along.

The Left is lost in a lost hope of impeaching Trump. Their suggestions get more outrageous by the day —it's hard to keep up with. By the time one pundit offers an interpretation, the next suggestion is already in draft. The problem is with order of strength. Usually we present our strongest arguments first. Usually the first strategies used are the strategies most likely to succeed. If so many things have failed this far into Trump's term, the likelihood of success isn't exactly high.

The Right—well, some of the Right—has been working harder than ever. The boring managers who can't keep an organization from floundering always hate the people who know what they're doing—like Trump. He just discovered how effective tariffs can be against the Chinese, why not try them against Mexico too!

The abortion debate is heating up to be hotter than it's ever been. While the Right-leaning states are banning abortion, Left-leaning states are legalizing types of abortion that formerly would never have passed into law. The more controversial this gets the more likely it will rise to the strongest conservative court we have seen in over half a century.

The Left and the "establishment" Right don't know how to respond. The workers and doers keep working and doing more things faster than the Left can make suggestions on how to stop them.

Cadence of Conflict: Asia, June 3

The "Symphony *Asian Mad Scientist Theorem*"** continues to play out. Trump engaged North Korea in talks that led to a calm without North Korea changing its DNA. Trump eventually reminded North Korea what everyone knew would be necessary to reach an agreement and North Korea stomped off.

Now, Trump comes off a marathon of wider-scope talks with China and continues to talk about talk, while the message is sent more clearly to China every day. China already knows what will be necessary to reach an agreement, its ambitions otherwise are classic Imperial-Confucian wishful thinking.

Over the weekend, the US and China exchanged insults at the International Institute for Strategic Studies in Singapore. America isn't gonna' tip-toe around China anymore! And, China will risk any and every cost and will defeat everyone who stands in the way! They sure told each other! We can't say China didn't warn us, just like China warned the world before the victorious Korean armistice and before China's great and splendid invasion of Vietnam.

Don't think for a second that Trump doesn't care about Japan. If he really didn't care about Japan—if he truly enjoyed the missiles recently launched by "Rocket Man"—he wouldn't say so on camera. Remember, everything he says is being closely watched by a large and volatile North Korean neighbor which believes that everyone believes everything published in the press.

No matter how much anyone warns China of the dangerous pinball machine game it's bouncing around inside of, they won't change because China only ever and always remains true to its Imperial-Confucian values. Those values can and will never include "capitulating to outside demands". China just won't change, you see.

Encore of Revival: America, June 10

One of the best-kept secrets in America is that tariffs discourage imports; if we raise tariffs, imports go down. Another best-kept secret is that if imports go down, domestic jobs go up. These two secrets are so well-kept that not even Senate Republicans know. They think that the same amount of imports will keep flowing in, even with tariffs. They think tariffs will not make consumers want to buy American-made goods again.

Even better-kept is the secret that tariffs discourage certain things in the country that makes the goods. When threatened with tariffs if "irregular" immigration wasn't stopped their side of the border, Mexico suddenly stopped illegal immigration previously said to be unstoppable. This comes as such a revolutionary surprise, perhaps we should consider that threatening tariffs on the sun could stop global warming! Tariffs seem capable of doing things no one imagined, after all.

Another well-kept secret is that America's government has its need to follow rules. Long, long ago, we all knew that the government has to play by certain rules. But, somewhere during the Obama years, we seem to have forgotten. Impeaching a president doesn't remove him from office; the House impeaches, but the Senate has to hold a trial before a president can be removed. Clinton was impeached and he stayed in office. Apparently Nancy Pelosi's voters didn't know that. So, she explained it to them. With all the well-kept secrets in the country, one has to wonder: *Why didn't "Nervous Nancy" Pelosi just try to impeach Trump, then act surprised that he stayed president?* She might have gotten more votes that way. Such lying theatrics wouldn't have worked ten years ago, but times are changing!

Cadence of Conflict: Asia, June 10

Chinese rhetoric spiked over recent weeks. They made threats. Trump made threats. They made more threats. Trump and Xi are BFF, just like Xi and Putin, but Xi and Putin are BFF-er. Now, we move toward quiet action. If China stops exporting "rare earth metals" to the US, the US would simply get them from somewhere else. "Rare" means many countries can get them, but few actually do because China does it so much.

The US is selling several tanks and tank-buster rockets to Taiwan. Beijing isn't happy—about the $2 Billion in weapons sales to Taiwan, but also because of the people who publicly express memory of what happened 30 years ago at Tienanmen Square.

Around the time Taiwan's primaries finish, the US launches its first Ford-class carrier in October, larger than a Nimitz. It still has a year of training and won't be commissioned until 2022.

Encore of Revival: America, June 17

The US could be looking at war on at least three fronts—as if things heating up in the Far East weren't enough. Two oil tankers were bombed in the Middle East and the Arab Prince blames Iran. The US claims to have evidence. Now, Senator Lindsey Graham is calling for war in Cuba to curb war with Venezuela.

All this international conflict is outshining the Left's ever weakening calls against Trump. But, the Left doesn't give up easily.

The summary of Robert Mueller's argument against Trump is that Trump tried to stop an investigation known to be fake. A group of people started a fake investigation against Trump, they broke the law, along with customary rules and ethical precedent. Mueller thinks Trump tried to stop this lawless, no-rules, fake investigation. Because of that, Trump "interfered with justice"?

Financially, the term for Mueller's side of the argument is called a "hostile takeover". That happens when one company wants to buy another company. The buying company just lies and makes false accusations until the other company is weak, then everyone says, "Well, I guess there is no choice except for the one company to get what it wants and buy the other."

If Trump had a kind of "technical foul" in stopping Mueller's fraudulent investigation, it would be Mueller, not Trump, who would have obstructed justice for creating the unlawful situation in the first place.

Democrats want the documents, hoping that the people won't see the deeper matters of justice and who started the baseless fight, rather than honoring the man who ended a fight that never should have started to begin with.

Cadence of Conflict: Asia, June 17

Trump's so-called "trade war" with China was never any failed attempt at relations. It was a way to get American companies out of China before the inevitable crud hit the fan. With Hong Kong's government ignoring it's people, we can see Trump's wisdom with China.

One million people in a population of just over 7 million protested a Beijing-backed extradition law in Hong Kong. Protests continued all week until a second, larger march returned one week later. What in the world is happening in the Far East? To understand Hong Kong, first take a look at Taiwan.

Much like the *Asian Mad Scientist Theorem*** for North Korea, consider the *Taiwan Schedule Theorem*, as follows: Unknown to the world, China has a military expansion schedule which requires possession of Taiwan. By a certain time, Beijing wants to use Taiwan's harbors to anchor China's Navy. Anything that threatens or delays that schedule causes China to take more extreme steps elsewhere, in fact anywhere, anyway. This isn't truth; it's a *theorem* that explains a lot.

For example, the DPP being elected in 2016 meant a slow in China's schedule for Taiwan—according to this theorem. That led Beijing to lean on Taiwan's allies, making them break off formal relations with Taipei.

With this theorem in mind, the goal of the US would, then, be to make as many disruptions with China's "Taiwan schedule" as possible, provoking China to exhaust its "other" ways to respond to schedule delays. Trade would be one way China could respond to schedule delays. But, the US trade war already removed "trade" as way to retaliate.

Another way China expands its power is through unofficial loans. Sri Lanka had to surrender a strategic sea port to China because of debt. Moreover, if countries borrow Chinese money off the books, then government bond values are inaccurate. Under-the-table lending is another rout China can take if the "Taiwan schedule" gets delayed, but that's been exposed and won't be so easy in the future.

China's getting boxed-in and Taiwan absorption seems farther and farther away.

With snowballing US-Taiwan cooperation— including the FBI scene last week, also including the $2 Billion in arms sales—China will see more delays. Protesting the G20 set for June 28, 2019 in Osaka would be another way Beijing could retaliate for delays in absorbing Taiwan. But, Trump already promised tariffs on yet another $300 Billion in goods if Xi Jinping doesn't show.

Chinese ambassadors to G20 countries are promoting anti-US sentiment. Will those countries be likely to side with China against the US just because a Beijing ambassador told them what to do? Even Hong Kongers don't like Beijing telling their CEO what to do. Perhaps Beijing doesn't know that. Perhaps Beijing knows, but doesn't care. Perhaps everyone "kowtowing" to China's demands over the last 40 years has led the Chinese to believe they are more influential than they really are. Beijing doesn't seem to be aware of where it stands with international opinion. But, it might find out soon.

Does any Chinese president show up where he is not welcome? Think about that...

With Trump's G20 threat in place, if Xi Jinping shows up at G20 where his anti-US diplomacy efforts "un-welcomed" him, then people will think he succumbs to threats and is weak. If he doesn't show, then Trump will lecture China publicly about "keeping a schedule" while Xi's country faces tariffs on $300 Billion of goods, and Xi will be seen as weak. More importantly, with new tariffs, China would be even less able to retaliate to delays in the "Taiwan schedule". Either way, drama over G20 exhausts China and leads to a checkmate.

If Taiwan is considered a playing "card", then it is a "trump" card, as they say. Taiwan might be a chess piece, but not one that gets sacrificed. Taiwan may be the pawn-turned-queen to hold the king in check at the end game.

Now, consider Hong Kong, where a "to other countries including China" extradition law brought out 1 Million Hong Kongers in protest, twice. CEO Carrie Lam outright ignored the protestorstwice. She's sad—not about her proposed extradition law, but that the law is opposed. Ignoring 1/7th of the population when they march in the streets is a bad idea in any country, in any universe. But, Carrie doesn't care, thus reflecting the worldview of any Beijinger.

Taiwan responded by deciding that it would not cooperate with the Hong Kong extradition law, even if passed, until "human rights" were addressed and only if Hong Kong heeded the opinion of its people in choosing whether to pass the law. Without Taiwan's support, the largest—if not only—reason known to the public for the law has vanished. And, it's all because of Taiwan.

One important factor in the "Taiwan schedule" is the upcoming election. Things seemed to be leaning toward Mayor Han of Kaohsiung for the KMT-Nationalist party. But, the events in Hong Kong over the past week have weakened Han and almost certainly assured a second term for Taiwan's incumbent, President Tsai. That means only more delays in the "schedule"

If Beijing can't get a grip on Taiwan quickly, Beijing will tighten its grip on Hong Kong even more.

But, Hong Kong is small and already attached to the mainland and doesn't lend itself to much in the way of retaliation. Too many changes in Hong Kong law and countries will break treaty with Hong Kong and the "Asia's World City" show will be finished. Once Hong Kong is no longer sufficient for Beijing to lash out over delays with Taiwan, the only retaliation left will be to invade Taiwan. That was Washington's goal all along—a fight for Taiwan that requires Pentagon intervention—and long-term presence after—and China started it.

Beijing might be willing for a pro-unification candidate to win Taiwan's election. But, if other things crowd in too quickly—say the US normalizes with Taiwan—the 2020 election wouldn't help the "Taiwan schedule" either way. Beijing needs to give Washington a reason not to formalize ties with

Taipei, and so far they haven't. G20 will decide a lot; China voting "absent" will decide a lot more a lot more quickly. Based on this *Taiwan Schedule Theorem*, expect more jeers and insults leading up to G20, from both sides, at the end of this month and expect Beijing to try every way to tighten its grip on Hong Kong.

Encore of Revival: America, June 24

Our president called off an invasion that could have been what the *Bay of Pigs* was to JFK. We were on the brink of nuclear war with Russia 58 years ago, and we didn't even know it! What is the value of a human life compared to a drone? Isn't the purpose of drones to spare human life? Some would use the loss of a drone as an excuse to end human life, but not our president.

Strategy and navigation that win always elude the untrained mind. What seems to most people like the way to win is precisely how to lose. What seems idiotic to most people is the only way to win. Trump's ongoing fight against establishments in both Asia and Washington prove who is on which side of the "which way is wise" debate. One of those important, counter-intuitive strategies is *mercy*.

"To err is human; to forgive, divine," wise words, courtesy Alexander Pope. There are many traps in politics. It is an indication of scruples and wisdom to know how to navigate through them. Refusing to murder in vengeance of a downed drone is no sign of weakness, but a sign of strength. Trump did far worse to Iran than any could imagine: *He showed mercy.*

That was just the beginning.

Cadence of Conflict: Asia, June 24

We are not headed to a Second Cold War. We are not at risk of heading to a Second Cold War. We are traveling at trans-warp speed toward the First Flash War. It will start and end quickly, laying the groundwork for WWIII and FWII to follow.

These pieces of our times are important to distinguish. Different analysts with different levels of understanding of history are trying their best to explain our times. To a novice—either to history or to the West or to the East—who just begins to understand, it may seem like we are headed toward Cold War II.

China and the US are in a growing conflict on the surface, but Russia is whispering in China's ear. Russia wants the same old thing. The US is generally unaware of Russia's intent or dismisses it.

China thinks that the US wants to retain power. China wants to rise, so Beijing feels the need to "beat back" the US.

The US knows China wants to rise and doesn't mind. The US wants to step back, but knows China is an undisciplined bully—lawless and doesn't respect human rights. So, the US feels the need to "beat down" China to make Beijing behave.

The US takes the approach of protectionism and innovation—tariffs and moving manufacturing back home. China takes the approach of its domineering culture and copying others—both doomed to fail.

One of the Chinese's biggest complaints used to justify their military aggression in the South Sea is American presence. The claim is that the US has 180 military bases throughout East Asia, rephrased "near China". Because of this, China calls America the "aggressor" and, like the burglar who thinks society stole from him first, says its military response is justified.

The US has been in many of those places since the end of WWII and after the Korean War. The Chinese didn't know about this US presence because their surveillance tech wasn't good enough. Once China reverse-engineered and stole designs for enough Western tech—because they still don't know how to invent it on their own—they started to see that Americans had been their the whole time.

The "Second Coming Cold War" argument is flawed because we've already been in such a "cold" standoff for seven decades. That's how Beijing interprets it anyway, and now the Chinese want to heat things up.

Consider the contradiction. For over 70 years, Americans have been quietly watching the seas. They didn't harass fishermen. They didn't aim missiles and launch threats. They didn't attempt to ram into other boats. They never tried to deny passage through international waters. China has done all these things, but not the US—in 70 years! So, because of that, the US is the aggressor? That's Beijing-style thinking anyway. And, that way of thinking is what Washington feels the need to defeat before it gets any bigger.

This week documented a Chinese general committing two "no-nos". Firstly, he commented on the social structure of Hong Kong—military leaders are supposed to remain outside of politics. Secondly, the thus proven military government of China thus also proved disdain for the law it must abide by. Motive is one vital burden of proof in a conviction. Not only had Beijing meddled where it wasn't allowed, but we now have an established motive.

Encore of Revival: America, July 1

It's the Art of the Deal. Trump and his work in East Asia at G20 upstaged political niggling in the US. His visit to North Korea upstaged G20. Meeting with the estranged Xi Jinping at Osaka—after rumors of Xi not showing and/or not talking, being the first sitting president to cross the Koreas' border into the north at the DMZ, then accompanying Kim inside for talks on the other side of the border in the south—this is bigger than anything going on in the Democratic presidential debates.

Meanwhile in Washington, the focus should remain on the courts. Justices are no longer divided evenly and clearly, neither along lines of politics nor judicial philosophy. Justice Gorsuch sided with the Constitution against the should-be Conservatives.

In politics, "Conservative vs Liberal" is about social tradition and whether to guarantee due process to ones opponents. On the Court, "Conservative vs Liberal" is about whether to strictly apply law as written vs trying to rule each case as an indirect way of "creating" new law. Both sides of the recent gun crime case voted on party lines—to let criminals walk vs to punish criminals—all except Gorsuch, who sided with the Liberals only because the law was too vague. It seems that Gorsuch is the only judicial Conservative on the court, while the rest seem to be Republican or Democratic activists.

We are looking at a third term for President Trump, along with a sixth Republican-appointed justice on the Supreme Court.

Happy Independence Week!

Cadence of Conflict: Asia, July 1

The Korean DMZ is the hottest new place to socialize! Dear Leaders charge to the border to shake hands. Presidents line up early to get a good spot. Few diplomatic maneuvers or promises on trade can compete with the political electricity and friendship found at the one border in Asia that has no military.

Trump's visit to Kim Jong-Un on his way home paid a great honor to the leader who was *not* at the G20 summit. Peace in Korea means a harder sell for countries seeking something else.

Leaders at G20 smiled for the camera and acted like best friends forever, reassuring their citizens back home. But, a bridge that spans 90% of a river is neither a bridge nor a dock, it's just an obstruction. Trade is on the table. Trump made a gesture without tread, allowing American companies to work with Huawei, as long as they don't help Huawei in the ways Trump claims Huawei continues to threaten security. Xi smiled, but didn't seem impressed.

Hong Kong protests have continued four weekends in a row.

If we look at the Hong Kong protests from the view of the *Asian Mad Scientist Theorem***, everything makes perfect sense. Experimentation with North Korea is finished and moved onto China. Now, it's time to see what happens when attempting to impose tyranny onto an unarmed, peaceful, free-thinking, free-speaking people.

Their main reaction was to petition G20 nations the week of the G20 summit. China has declared Hong Kong to be an internal matter that will not be discussed at G20. This creates a dilemma similar to the line between an internal family matter vs the kids banging on the neighbors' door to report domestic violence. If internal matters escalate to a certain point, then can't not become external matters.

Grenville Cross should be investigated for unhealthy ties to Beijing. Being the director of public prosecutions starting in 1997, when Hong Kong was handed over to Beijing, and with his recent "opinion" piece*, more of a political rebuke of the protestors, he is operating as Beijing's mouthpiece and overlooked one important part of Hong Kong's Basic Law—mainly that Beijing *may never, ever, ever* interfere. He should be investigated as an accomplice with a means and a now evident motive.

The Huawei FedEx package returned to Sascha
Segan doesn't seem to be a lash-out at China, but
a lash-out at Trump.

*If Hong Kong's extradition bill protesters want to
defend the rule of law, they must also be prepared
to face it, June 26, 2019, South China Morning Post

Encore of Revival: America, July 8

Trump's tanks were unimpressive—that's what Russian pundits think, anyway. Bringing out these old, beat-up, partially-disassembled relics of past victory and sacrifice proves nothing important. Parades should tout the latest, most intimidating, most high-tech muscle the military can muster. By all those standards, Trump's parade flopped. Instead, he celebrated America's heart and heritage—all things unimpressive in the eyes of Russians pining for their old imperial days of glory gone bye.

The Left, on the other hand, thought it was too much. JFK and Clinton celebrating bravery with marches and fly-overs were good, until Trump did it, then they weren't. Perhaps next year's Independence Day could host a bilateral talk between the Left and their recently-estranged Russian comrades.

Russia and America's Left weren't the only ones trying to tell Trump what to do. A leak from Britain's Daily Mail shows disdain from the ambassador of the failed administration. Some suspect an attempt to influence fast-approaching election politics in the UK by painting Trump as the villain. More likely is a rogue, self-appointed hero who doesn't like the manners of movers and shakers, pretending that his experience as an ambassador means his personal value for fecklessness should "trump" the White House, as it were.

Newt was the most out-spoken for Trump. He thinks not invading Iran was smart and that Trump is making all the right decisions on his successful path to re-election 2020.

Some important things happened in Civil Rights. The Republicans missed two great chances on these.

California finally passed a law, more or less, seeming to clarify what kinds of haircuts are natural for Black people. Though it doesn't fit with the conventional Right of 20 years ago—always turning away from "touchy-feely" laws—it's about time. What is wrong with Black people wearing dreads, anyway? Dreads are the easiest way for Black people wear their hair if they don't go to the barber every other day. Why was this political and why was the law needed? The reason is probably because most White people don't know that Black people need an entirely different kind of clippers at the barber shop. Some sad Republican politician who didn't know as much just might complain about Cali, then lose his seat in 2020.

A DA in Philly won't fine people in poverty beyond restitution anymore. Crime will be prosecuted, of course. Damages must be paid, of course. But, there's no point in fining someone $1,000 who can't pay rent and barely affords a car that's worth less. Such a fine would effectively make the sentence an eviction. Current laws might as well say, "This crime is punishable by two weeks income if you're middle class, an afternoon round of golf if you're rich, and eviction if you're poor." Why didn't Republicans make criminal and traffic fines proportional to income already? With the income gap gaping so wide, fines shouldn't be measured in dollars, but in percentages. Some Republican politician probably won't know that either.

Speaking of Republicans, Justin Amash of Grand Rapids' district in Michigan took Independence Day to announce his independence from the RNC. His statement appeared as an Op-Ed in the Washington Post. Maybe he'll be the one to start the People's Party.

Whether it's the communists in Russia and America quibbling about tanks in parades, getting Republicans to get along, being aware that Black and White people have different hair, or considering that flat fine rates aren't fair, America has a lot to learn. We're learning, we've come a long way in 243 years, we're not there yet, but we're inching along alright. We're inching along.

Cadence of Conflict, Asia, July 8

China has been had. It has been had by Western freedom. It has been had by its own culture's psychopathology. It has been had by the concept of a promise—something the Chinese can't understand, let alone keep. It has been had by Marxist propaganda. And, it is still being had by its obsession with power.

British officials are turning their eyes toward Hong Kong. This is a move of revival in the English-speaking world. The English have a conscience. It is more than political smoke-blowing. Britain fully intends to protect the people of Hong Kong. And, they can do it because China has already reneged on a treaty registered with the United Nations.

China has difficulty understanding the concept of a promise. Living fully and wholly by the psychopathology of Gorgias—that all statements are lies and only rhetoric matters—the Chinese truly believe that their promise to not interfere with Hong Kong until 2047 is irrelevant trivia. They truly believe that if the world distrusts China for breaking treaty, it would be the world just looking for ways to be mean to poor, suffering, victimized

121

China. They truly believe that any "distrust" from the West, citing broken promises, would be pure propaganda from any and all, everywhere on Earth.

The British dealt with China for centuries. They must have at least suspected that China would break treaty. In fair honesty, by allowing a fifty year window, they showed high hopes that China would at least be capable of pretending to have a conscience for half a century. If China could lie to the world for fifty years and conceal its spite for any race lacking Han blood—if China could at least pretend to be nice for fifty years—then perhaps Hong Kong would be safe long after 2047. Britain gave China the benefit of the doubt.

But, China didn't make it fifty years, not even half that.

Call it temptation. Call it the "Tienanmen fix". China can't not oppress and boss and dominate. From Beijing, Hong Kong calls, begging, "Oppress me! Oppress me!"

From Xi Jinping's perspective is one of power. He believes that the Russian Communist downfall of 1989 happened because the Communists didn't oppress enough. It never occurs to him that people do not overthrow governments that they trust—but to a psychopath, all statements are lies and all protests are propaganda. People would only hate an oppressive government, so they think, because someone told them to.

Hong Kong knows differently. Though they do not have complete self-rule, they do have free speech, free markets, free press, and free religion. To them, China stinks, and not only from the pollution of mismanagement.

Still, China wants to force its embrace upon the free people of Hong Kong. The legal justice system has a term for criminals who force their love on unwilling victims. In that scenario, everyone knows who everyone is.

Like an alcoholic claiming that alcohol is the medicine, China sees voluntary support as a threat —as a lack of power—and that power is the cure for power resisted. China has been had by everyone, its own vices above all else.

Encore of Revival: America, July 15

Justice Roberts doesn't believe that the citizenship question in the upcoming census is about voting rights. He's right, it probably isn't. A more believable reason might have been to confirm the accuracy of immigrant statistics from other Federal reports. A better census question would have been multiple choice: citizen, green card, other visa, and entry not requiring visa—nothing incriminating about that. Putting the question on a separate form from the rest of the census form would skew the data to protect privacy. But, SCOTUS wouldn't allow the question as presented for the reason as defended.

We have two big issues with this ruling. First, if census questions are too invasive, people won't answer them, then the data is less accurate. Second, remember: The Supreme Court always votes in favor of the Court, more than Right or Left politics, more than constitutionalism or idealism. And, as we should expect from hard-working law school grads, supreme justices love to penalize sloppy homework.

If we wanted to know Roberts's politics, the defense should have provided a better defense. Trump shouldn't have let his lawyers give lame reasons for relevant questions because the true reasons are good enough: The government wants to know the accuracy of other reports. Now, those other reports will be collected, collaborated, and cross-referenced instead, which might have been a better rout in the first place.

The Democrats enjoyed the younger generation of voters accusing anything and everything of being about racism, even when it wasn't. It came in handy as a wild carded, one-shot-for-all silver bullet for rebutting opposition to Obama. It helped them get elected under the auspices of fighting a never-ending battle that had to continue. But, when one such young person got elected, it messed with the non-democratic rank-and-file culture of the so-called Democratic party. Now, Pelosi and AOC are in a cat fight. The problem is that people care. It's not news, it's just politics as usual. Maybe it's a nice wake-up call to what is usual in Washington.

Just as usual is the scandalous underbelly of Washington, including Epstein. When he was caught up in scandals with Democrats, he didn't matter. Now that they can't keep their underage pimp afloat, the salvage operation in the

Washington spin-control department wants to tie Epstein to Trump to at least get some return for their great loss. They'll have to find someone to replace him now. And, they'd at least like to say the same for Trump, but they can't.

Cadence of Conflict: Asia, July 15

China's recent obsession with arresting Canadians is easier to understand and predict if it is seen as an attempt to alienate US allies from the US. Based on this, we can expect mistreatment of other US citizen allies in the future. They did something similar with an Australian back in January. By lashing out at citizens of US allies, China—more than likely—hopes to make those countries regret being friends with the US...

...because that works in Chinese culture's inside baseball.

Something about Chinese-Confucian culture is obsessed with "the group" and "uniform conformity". When someone steps "out of line"— whatever the groupthink happens to have decided "the line" is this afternoon—others within that culture instinctively begin to attack that person like hyenas attack an isolated impala in the wild. It's almost as if they are governed by a hypnotic auto-think. Small charges, snaps, and bites slowly creep in from any and every side until the group kills and devours whoever tried to be different.

This is exactly what China has done to Taiwan's allies. Most of them caved. Senator Rubio lashed out at El Salvador for abandoning Taiwan last August when the trend became annoyingly obvious. Since it worked with them, maybe China thinks it will work with the English-speaking world.

But, the Chinese only learn "Chinglish" at best, whether with language or with culture. There attempt will only backfire and that will explain the members of the coming alliance that defeats China in the fast-approaching scuffle. And, it will explain the coming alliance that nations just east of China will soon deepen with the English-speaking world, as well as the growing alienation between English-America and Latin-America. But, that won't be seen for another decade.

Encore of Revival: America, July 22

Washington is all excited because this week Mueller is scheduled to testify, again, about a report he already handed in. If the report had said enough on its own then there would be no need for him to testify, again. Democrats are all excited, but not as excited as Senator Graham, who plans to launch his own investigation investigation. While Washington is distracted with theatrics of Russians and the "fab four", a much deeper problem is swelling, one which will not escape Trump's tenure unchanged: social media.

Social media giants are out of control. One current argument on the table is to make Google's "index" public.

This "index" is Google's inside stockpile of information that a "Google search" queries. Right now, it's on lockdown and no one can access it without going through Google. Making it public would allow anyone to use it—if they know the right code, which code monkeys could learn. And, that's where the trouble is...

Publicizing Google's search index would be difficult to prove because it would need a new computer language—or API—to access. What's to keep Google from making that API language too difficult to use? And, what's to ensure the same idiots in Washington who tried to ram SOPA & PIPA down everyone's throats—or wondered if Hillary wiped her server "with a cloth"—would know whether Google is making the API too difficult to use?

It could be done. It would need oversight. It should apply to Yahoo, Microsoft, and any other publicly traded tech giant with a search index. And, it would be a game changer.

According to Bloomberg, Google gets over 90% of all search traffic; Microsoft's Bing at second place gets under 3%. That's a lot of power to be in just one place.

While the current thinkers have "thunk" up this as the way to regulate Google under laws governing "public utilities", there's another important argument to consider. Google's search index isn't an index about Google's own intellectual property —Google's search index is an index about private information owned by everyone. So, the real question is whether it should be legal to "index the public", which is essentially what Google does. If it's legal to "index the public", then of course the public should have access to that index, duh.

Cadence of Conflict: Asia, July 22

In the singing, fake-smiling scenes of Uyghurs in reeducation camps in China, the Chinese expect the world to be swayed to believe they are happy. That's how Chinese view it with each other—they fake-smile at each other and buy the lie because they hope other people buy into their own fake smiles. The Chinese have no idea that Westerners know when they are truly happy and truly not, being able to tell a fake smile when we see one—or two or ten thousand.

If Chinese Foreign Ministry spokesman Geng Shuang and China's *Global Times* tabloid editor Hu Xijin are right—that the White House shouldn't get "the credit" for China's sinking economy—then China would be thankful, but they aren't. It's just more Chinese chicken-chest thumping. So focused on forcing the world to love them back, the Chinese Communist Party and their media puppets are unaware of how they come across to the rest of the world that actually does not need to bend to their demands.

Xi Jinping is the modern Hitler. He calmly talks of peace, claims to not want war, then rouses his sleeping anger to growl that he will use force if necessary. The concentration-brainwashing camps are set up and well-marketed. Everyday shows more unapologetic expansionism upon territories who want nothing to do with China. Symphony's *Asian Mad Scientist Theorem*** is proving too accurate for comfort and Hong Kong doesn't want any part.

China might as well get used to this happening in Taiwan, though they won't accept that the Taiwanese won't accept Chinese rule any more than Hong Kongers. The difference is that Taiwan has missiles and a military. And, multiple times throughout half a millennium of adversity, Taiwan is only conquered by the enormous mainland when the enormous mainland is already conquered by something else. Mayor Han of Kaohsiung, the KMT-Nationalist contender in the upcoming presidential election in Taiwan, has already been defeated for the populist he is. The election isn't over, but then again it kind of already is.

Hong Kong has drawn so much attention that Taiwan is looking into asylum avenues, the EU is voicing support for Hong Kong protesters' demands, and Britain is looking to support not just Hong Kong, but also Taiwan. China, not having learned from the opium wars, has once again been cruel to the little kid in the Far East,

oblivious to the anger awakened in his older
brother in the West.

133

Encore of Revival: America, July 29

The anti-Trump spin machine is in full swing. It's difficult to believe that 47% of Americans want him impeached by trusting only one pollster—Fox News, which wrongly predicted his non-election. It's even more difficult to believe that polls, in general, aren't being doctored when someone managed to anonymously change the presidential seal on a background screen into a Russian eagle that golfs. These things suggest a concerted effort to undermine the president. But, we already knew about that, didn't we?

Trump can't be labeled as the only source of drama in America. The economy is up, but so are spending and debt. Jobs are returning to America while manufacturing flees China as fast as peace is fleeing Hong Kong—which China blames on the US. The UK has a new prime minister who is just as opposed by the outgoing administration as Trump is opposed by Washington's still outstanding swamp.

The contrived Russianewsgategate fiasco wasn't a bombshell, it was more of a fizzle and pop, and its biggest explosion may be its backfire. Now that the fizzling and popping are finished popping and fizzling, the investigation investigations are starting up; Comey is the lead person of great interest.

Like bad habits, bad people don't go away easily. It takes time and effort. Bad people lie just because they know they can't win any other way. And, it takes having a head in the right place to know when that's happening.

Cadence of Conflict: Asia, July 29

China says that Hong Kong CEO Carrie Lam may not resign because she must remain in power to clean up the mess China started and blames on her. Albeit, staying in power to clean up her scapegoat mess is impossible because cleaning up that mess requires her to resign as the people demanded. The "mess" includes her being there in the first place—because her election was not from self-governance as Hong Kongers were promised in 1984. The mess also includes China saying who may and may not resign—because China doesn't get a say about one grain of sand in Hong Kong until 2047.

The whole problem goes back to China's inability to not meddle. A Beijing-managed group based in Shenzhen has been carefully researching and observing the developments in Hong Kong so that Beijing can know how to properly respond—whatever that's supposed to mean. Make no mistake, they aren't trying to understand how to govern a free people or understand the reasonable requests of a free and self-motivated economy. They aren't trying to learn whatever wisdom might have made the West so rich and powerful in the first place. No, Beijing is on a mission to Sinicize Hong Kong out of being Hong Kong.

The current task is to figure out how to "disappear" 2 million Hong Kongers without the world noticing. Hong Kong's police under-reported the 2 million turnout; they'll probably under-report the number of "disappeared" people as well, and they need research to make it sound convincing. If the protests had happened in Xinjiang, Beijing wouldn't need to do such research because the world wouldn't be watching because making 2 million people disappear in Xinjiang was never a problem in the past. And, that's what Hong Kongers rightly fear.

Beijing's research narrative presumes that Hong Kongers only fear being "Xinjianged" because some phantom, invisible Western influence influenced them. They have no proof of this, but that's Beijing's presumption. If there's a problem, it must be America's fault. So, Beijing's approach is to sneak around and spy from the shadows until this phantom "influence monster" from the evil West shows its face. That's Beijing's plan to solve the Hong Kong problem.

Now, there's constitutional discussion about where and how Hong Kong's "Basic Law" allows military intervention from China, namely if Hong Kong's government asks. But, the whole discussion misses the whole point—that Hong Kong's Basic Law is based on the Sino-British Joint Declaration of 1984 of non-interference from Beijing. Beijing already interfered by not allowing self-governance in Hong Kong as promised. Not letting Carry Lam resign is yet another violation of that promise and premise. So, technically, the law beneath the Basic Law has already been dissolved. And, Beijing only incriminates itself further by claiming that promises made in the past don't need to be kept because they are in the past.

Pay attention because, while Taiwan is a linchpin that will bring America into war with China, Hong Kong is the linchpin that will bring the UK and Europe along with it.

Encore of Revival: America, August 5

Tariffs and trade headlines aren't about trade or tariffs; they are about Trump. The trade war with China isn't about China having taken US jobs since before the 1980s, it's "Trump's trade war". The poor American farmers who planted crops to suit the Chinese are all beside themselves. A bad environment—whether in weather or economics—is the new normal and farmers are being told the same thing as American companies that depend on China: get used to it and look elsewhere.

America's economy can't be dependent on China because China is not dependable. Look at the self-contradiction of someone who says otherwise. Trump's former economic adviser, Gary Cohn, says in one sentence that China was going to take down its own economy anyway, then in another sentence says that US trade policy is backfiring. Which is it? Was China going to do all this anyway or did the US initiate something that backfired? Both can't be true at the same time.

Either the US affected China's economic policy or it didn't—for better or worse. Claiming that we didn't make a difference while also claiming that we made a difference that backfired doesn't indicate a well-considered economic framework; it indicates someone shooting in the dark, trying to find any argument that will convince people to dislike Trump. After all, America's economy was wonderful while it made China rich, but once the US economy stopped serving China, it wasn't a "US trade war", it was "Trump's trade war".

Many Trump critics believe Trump supporters are stupid, but they still try to use reason to persuade Trump supporters. This is another self-contradiction, adding to the self-contradicting reasoning. Even if self-contradiction could persuade Trump supporters to abandon him, there would be no place to turn. Democratic infighting is at an all-time high. It's almost as if the Democrats want to lose the 2020 election, pretending to fight valiantly while they do. But, that wouldn't be anything new. They have been doing that with human rights and civil rights for decades.

Cadence of Conflict: Asia, August 5

If one were to guess what was going on between Trump and Kim, internal politics of North Korea would explain it all. Korea is no exception to East Asia's history of ongoing domination quarreling. Kim is not universally loved within his own government. The military is constantly at his back door and he must squash mutinies constantly. Pomp and acting like he's the "military man" makes it hard for his enemies within to rally ill will against him.

Also, Trump has commented that many things are going on with North Korea behind the scenes— things which remain beyond the paparazzi watch of the Western presses. When Trump indicates no objection to the non-nuclear missile launches in North Korea, it almost seems as if Trump knows Kim is doing something the rest of the West doesn't know about. For all we know, the number and frequency of non-nuclear missile tests could be a kind of Morse code only known to Trump and Kim. Given what has been publicly told, that would not be impossible. This only leads us to conclude that we can't conclude anything about what's happening in North Korea so far; there have just been too many jokers added to the deck.

Then, there's China, China, and also China.

When it comes to raising public support for Western action against China, China is its own worst PR enemy.

China keeps doing the same thing. Beijing's solution to rejection is to incite more rejection. Beijing's solution to resistance is to give excuse for more resistance. It's in a self-destructing insanity tailspin—paranoid of invisible enemies, justifying interfering in Hong Kong under the auspices that Hong Kong was already interfered in by the West.

That's what this is all about, by the way. The whole reason Beijing accuses Taiwan and the US of causing the Hong Kong riots is to build the case that "Hong Kong was already interfered with", and therefore sending in China's military to stop the protests would not violate the Basic Law. The problem is that the Basic Law does not grant China permission to use military force against unarmed Hong Kong citizens on the basis of "Western interference". But, the Chinese don't understand the concept of "lawfulness" anyway. They just come up with whatever excuse sounds sophisticated enough to seem smarter than everyone else and thereby hypnotize the public into compliance.

China wants to blame the US and Trump won't give China one single excuse to be twisted into so-called proof. Trump treads cautiously, but he is neither callous nor oblivious. His silence should be a warning to China that he is no fool. Sadly, China will take his silence to mean that he has caved into Beijing's aggression and the Chinese military will only grow more overconfident than it already is. But, choices of the past four decades suggest that may have been the plan all along.

The tipping point is upon us. If China's warship crashed into a Taiwan freighter on accident, then there would be no reason to fear or respect China's Navy because their crew can't steer. The alternative is to interpret it as an act of war. China doesn't consider either because an angry bully in blamer-mode doesn't consider others, not even how others can or will respond.

Encore of Revival: America, August 12

Every time there's a shooting, everyone uses emotion to say everyone was right and everyone else was wrong. "More killing, so all the rest of you should agree with my politics, dah!" It started with attitude. Mass shootings only indicate an already-divided country. People either demand guns everywhere or guns denied or some combination thereof; no one argues in favor of training the militia.

The Second Amendment guaranteed the right for all to own and carry firearms because all were obligated to be trained in the militia. Liberals want none of it and so-called Conservatives want the arms with not a single word about militia training for all. But, militia training for all citizens would solve the problem, both the attitudes of potential shooters and the readiness of the general public. People with "mental problems" wouldn't be allowed in the militia and thereby wouldn't be able to own firearms. Denying weapons to the insane and unstable in that way would calm concerns of the Right.

The Right is concerned that the Left wants to force the Right to behave like they are part of the Left. With recent laws that punish people for not agreeing to LGBTQ speech patterns, who can blame them? With Universal Studios' *The Hunt* even having been filmed, who can blame the Right for feeling the need for self-defense? Still, we don't need massive gun ownership without training; we need the militia for all people. The militia is what the Right-Wing's precious Constitution calls for, but the Right-Wing has not. So, their fear of the Left, however justified, is well-earned.

Even in a Liberal utopia where everyone is filled with hatred, while all means of acting on such hatred have been removed, no one would be safe without public-wide training. The whole public needs to be trained to deal with every dangerous scenario, from a dictator's takeover to an invasion to a mass shooting. It's called the "militia" and it's the one thing neither extremist nor moderate of our polarized political spectrum even peeps about.

Cadence of Conflict: Asia, August 12

China instructs Hong Kong not to confuse restraint for weakness, notwithstanding that China is making that very mistake with the West in not sponsoring the demands of Hong Kongers that Hong Kong's government keep the Sino-British promise of 1984. China claims that the West has meddled in Hong Kong. The biggest problem with this argument isn't lack of evidence, though evidence is lacking. The bigger problem is *need*— the West wouldn't need to meddle in order to create the chaos we see in Hong Kong because China has already done more than enough. Balancing Hong Kong's unrest with China's interference, the math adds up.

As China poetically said of Hong Kong, a "blow from the sword of law is waiting for them in the future." China should heed its own words. But, we already knew China was incapable heeding any wisdom, including its own, which is probably why the West doesn't bother commenting anymore. After all that has happened, China recently had the lack of self-awareness to call its growing power a "peaceful rise" in defense of growing Australian concerns.

Taiwan is gearing up and arming up. Their new "Cloud Peak" missile can reach Beijing. It's mobile and in mass-production. It still pales in comparison to Beijing's aggression toward everyone, everywhere. But, Taiwan figures, at least an attack from Beijing would hurt in Beijing. But, Beijing's probably not capable of understanding that. So, the Taiwanese can't count on their Cloud Peak missiles as any kind of deterrent, only a disruptor to cripple and confuse and weaken sequential attacks from an attacker who struck first.

Encore of Revival: America, August 19

The nation is polarizing even more. The anti-Israel sentiment from some members of Congress is only one part. The Russianewsgategate scandal surfaces more evidence every day, but no one changes heart or mind on the matter. Portland protests have the same non-effect on persuading people to change sides, only mobilizing everyone.

Chris Cuomo is grossly annoyed by Limbaugh's nickname for him. Perhaps he thinks he's the only one allowed to get offended. Senator Lindsey "Gramnesty" wore his like a badge of honor and Andrea "Tarantula" Tantaros welcomed Rush as a guest on her show to explain the good humor of it all. At this point, it's unlikely Rush will be able to grace the ratings of Chris, who seems to be the only one with a nickname the rest of us aren't allowed to use.

While protests and extreme voices raise their volume, the only thing provoking people to switch sides are Liberals in the spotlight. It's not all—neither those in the spotlight or those switching sides. But, some of the dumber and loudest among the Left have made themselves such an embarrassment that many social-minded voters are starting to think that they will get more social justice from the Right.

The election has always been and remains in Trump's favor. China will lose the trade war, as well as the other war it was always going to instigate. Gun laws and abortion laws will strengthen in both directions. While the Right seems to have the advantage for now, neither Right nor Left has any clear path towards domination, only further polarity. There's no stopping it. Buckle up, grab your popcorn, and stay safe.

Cadence of Conflict: Asia, August 19

Conflicts with China are helping Taiwan. The trade war is driving manufacturing away from China toward Taiwan, Vietnam, and Burma, among others. China's travel ban on Taiwan for openly supporting the Hong Kong protests is pushing the Taiwanese to implement better visa privileges with other Asian nationals visiting Taiwan. Not only did last week's occupation of the Hong Kong International Airport break Western confidence in the Chinese "Special Administrative Region", the Hong Kong protests are even affecting business in Macau.

Why the protests? Where did it all start? Follow the money. Of the many factors, one of the best kept secrets around the world is the housing cost for local Hong Kongers. It's called "gentrification". Ordinary Hong Kong citizens can't afford even the least expensive homes without government subsidy in addition to living with family. A Hong Kong jail cell is larger that many homes.

That happened because Hong Kong's government, clearly under the thumb of Beijing, allows Mainland Chinese citizens to move into Hong Kong at such a high rate that new housing can't be built fast enough to keep residential costs affordable. Wealthy Chinese need a place to live, some place where they can enjoy life. They won't find anything nice enough within China proper, so they have to go somewhere with an economy created by the West—somewhere like Hong Kong. That way they can enjoy all the money of China without the lousy lifestyle. In their view, it would be cruel for Hong Kong not to let as many Chinese Mainlanders displace native Hong Kongers as fast as possible.

Protests are entering their eleventh week. One more week will begin a new record of 79 days from the Umbrella Movement in 2014.

Encore of Revival: America, August 26

The news media can't understand Trump. One of the reasons he uses so few words and repeats himself so often is to "sound-bite-proof" his statements. It's difficult to twist his words when he only spoke two of them in a 30 second period. The news media doesn't like not being able to cut and paste together a president's words to make him out to say whatever they want him to have said.

Since sound-bite clipping didn't work the last four years, this past week the media tried a new strategy: Pretend that they don't know what sarcasm is.

CNBC tried to paint Trump's sarcastic "I'm the chosen one" comment as self-aggrandizement. His sarcastic tone clearly communicates that the self-aggrandizement came from the presidents before him who thought themselves incapable of *not* funding China's Sinicization of the world. Anyone could and should have stopped China. Trump knows that. His tone said that. And, no less than 2 million Hong Kongers have risked their lives to prove just that.

Then we have "regrets". Does the president "regret" his trade dispute with China? Why shouldn't he? Everyone regrets everything, at least for some amount of time, given enough time. The news media keeps asking silly questions that deserve silly answers. Think about the question itself.

Is there a concrete reason to believe that President Trump has regrets about how trade is going with China? Did he say something attempting to reverse the dispute? Did he send a letter apologizing for something he did? Did he suddenly offer China massive concessions out of nowhere? What basis is there for thinking that Trump has "regrets" with China, other than the hope of succeeding with passive-aggression to paint Trump to be someone he is not?

Trump's "order" that American companies explore alternatives to China is not a power-grab, but a shot across the bow. As if fattening China in the first place didn't indicate enough lack of brains, most companies with half a hand at the helm should have long steered clear of China for all the chop. For those stragglers who still can't put two and two together, Trump's warning is a lighthouse. Danger lies ahead; adjust your course. This is gonna' be a big one.

But, all the media can do is complain about the
lighthouse. We'll see.

Cadence of Conflict: Asia, August 26

The Hong Kong police have lost public trust. They've cried, "Victim!" after their injuries were proven to be from self defense when they were the assailants. They illegally shot tear gas canisters as harmful projectiles in violation of international law and from windows high enough to kill someone if a canister landed on someone's head. One girl lost an eye because the police shot rubber bullets at the crowd at point blank range and one bullet passed through her protective face mask. Yet, the police claim that rubber bullets don't cause harm.

Now, peace turns to instant violence just because these police arrive. Or, perhaps it's because they arrive, then start pounding their batons against their shields as if they were Roman soldiers about to charge.

At the Yuen Long MTR Station in a somewhat remote part of Hong Kong's New Territories, protestors were loud, but not violent, until the police showed up. From well-earned fear, protestors tore up the place to block the police from blinding someone else. Trash cans and other furnishings were turned on side, fire extinguishers made a smokescreen, and the students pulled down a gate to block the way between themselves and the violent police of Hong Kong.

The greatest mistrust of Hong Kong police isn't their violence, but their inaction. The great criminals control the government. Perhaps protestors believe the police should enforce the Basic Law by forcefully unseating CEO Carrie Lam for violating the Sino-British Joint Declaration of 1984. But, they don't because they have become a tool of Beijing's interference, proven most by the usual Human Rights violations of Beijing.

But, Hong Kongers' fears are still greater, sharing an overlap with US President Trump. China wants to Sinicize the world, as the 2008 Olympics opening ceremony showed—as Hong Kong and Taiwan show—as America's economy shows.

As if Hong Kong's problems haven't shown enough about the greater threats looming over the world from the Far East, South Korea's vindictive administration keeps making trouble. This week, South Korea ended an intel sharing agreement with Japan, then stepped up military drills near an island disputed by Japan.

Encore of Revival: America, September 2

Comey's leaks are a matter of example and precedent. He must be prosecuted to the fullest extent possible because we can't have other FBI employees doing what he did—Republican or Democrat. More importantly, we must honor those FBI employees who could have done what he did, perhaps thought about doing what he did, but refused to break principles and protocol. For police, it's all about protocol.

The FBI director knew information that should not be given to the public. He knew it was wrong, what he did. So, he released it to the public through other people, lawyers and the news media. He claimed he did this—which he knew was wrong—because he loved his country and the FBI. If he loved the FBI, then he shouldn't have insulted the thousands of FBI employees who would surely be thrown in prison had they done the same thing.

If Comey is not prosecuted and fully indited, then Wikileaks founder Julian Assange shouldn't be either and Edward Snowden should receive the Presidential Medal of Freedom because their leaks showed actual corruption of people like Comey.

But, by not inditing Comey, we see clearly that the current Justice Department is run by double standards.

Double standards are a problem for courts, but they are a deadly epidemic for police. Once police are encouraged to live by a double standard, police brutality spreads. Not inditing Comey encourages and invites just that, spitting in the face of the good cops society needs.

If Comey believes his claim, that releasing this information was necessary, then he should voluntarily plead guilty and suffer for the sake of his cause, showing how much he truly cares about his country and its police. But, he won't because he's not a true believer. Thankfully, some still are.

Cadence of Conflict: Asia, September 2

Reuters broke the story. According to unnamed sources, Beijing refused to let Hong Kong's government grant free elections, withdraw the extradition bill, and crackdown on police brutality. If this report can be proven in court, a case could be made that Hong Kong is no longer under China's governance, already. Of course, China would never recognize such a ruling and a military conflict between China and the West would quickly ensue.

The West has slowly been inching forward in support of Western freedoms everywhere the West resides, including Hong Kong, and China has been ill prepared. Had Beijing anticipated the status quo, preventative measures would have been taken long ago. But, China doesn't understand the West, just as Beijing can't understand Westernized Hong Kong. So, "suspicion" is the emotional response to expect.

Well past the 79-day record of continued protests from the Umbrella Movement in 2014, the extradition protests are in their 13th week.

Turn of events included protestors setting large fires on police-related barricades and the police using blue die in water cannons, presumably to mark protestors for later action. This is a serious escalation on both sides. Far more importantly, but less likely to be noticed, protestors marched outside the Chinese military garrison, near Central on Hong Kong Island. This is a direct affront to Chinese control and, for that reason alone, the situation has never been more explosive, so to speak.

Hong Kong's miracle was that it was Western, but it was located in the Far East. This made it an overlap and a gem in the world. It was the convergence of extremes that made Hong Kong special. But, Confucian-Communist Chinese can't imagine that being Western would make a thing desirable. So, Beijing chalks-up Hong Kong's "greatness" to the idea that "it is Chinese".

In attempt to explain the protests, and without evidence, China has repeatedly accused the West of interfering in Hong Kong, which got its very value from already being Western. The greatest Western influence in Hong Kong came from Hong Kong itself. Reports of supposed Western financial backing for Hong Kong protests seem laughable to the West since they have been presented without a shred of anything remotely resembling a "paper trail"; it's mere surmise.

Far more importantly, since when did Beijing object to Western influence? Communism is Western. But, seeing that requires objective thought, something Confucian culture can't do.

Beijing supposes their must be someone behind the protests. In Confucian Chinese thinking, no one would oppose their great benevolence unless someone else told them to, and "objective thinking" is a mere myth. But, the West can't imagine anyone supporting the government of the Tienanmen Square massacre without brainwashing.

As Westerners, Hong Koners don't want to be brainwashed to support such a murderous government, neither does the rest of the West. So, with this past week, we can't expect the West not to interpret action against Hong Kong's protestors as a preemptive attack on the rest of Western civilization. World War veterans remember what happens when the West feels threatened. Still, no matter how much Hong Kong wants to, Beijing refuses to allow the only way to stop making Western culture feel like someone wants it to stop being Western.

Encore of Revival: America, September 9

British Parliament is essentially attempting to filibuster the Brexit referendum. PM Boris Johnson has been ordered by Parliament to agree with whatever decision comes from the EU—in which Johnson gets a vote and a veto. Maybe British Parliament should have gone on to instruct France not to veto an extension. The problem with this law is how non-specific it is, which is typical of posturing. Perhaps that's the best way for Johnson to legally "interpret" it. Johnson's main goal is to get a Brexit deal, which he believes will only be best if real fear of real failure is allowable. But, that's up to the British, so the rest of the would should grab a popcorn, not tell others what to do, and see how the theatrics end.

Why is America arguing about weather? Sabotage. Someone at NOAA gave the president a ridiculous forecast, that a hurricane would plow through a wall of heat and high pressure, which doesn't happen. Of course Dorian would turn right. But, someone advised him otherwise.

The president, who is not a meteorologist, then Tweeted caution and concern for Alabama, because someone at NOAA so advised, when everyone else at NOAA knew better. This is the work of someone trying to undermine the president. He's fired people who were wrong in the past, he should also fire the advisor who made the prediction that was as wrong as it was ridiculous.

The economy is doing well, contrary to the best efforts of the bank. Don't blame Trump for the Chinese trade war prices; blame the companies. Over 80% of our clothing and over half of our shoes are made in China. Whatever happened to cause that, Trump is fixing it. If we don't like the road of all things made in China, then don't do it again, and don't blame the cleaning lady.

Cadence of Conflict: Asia, September 9

The missile issues in North Korea have too much unknown about them to formulate a clear opinion. From reports, Kim has indeed kept his promise, though he has violated seemingly less significant UN sanctions. Japan is on alert. Trump doesn't seem to care. If we made a stack of American clothes made in China, then stacked what we don't know about the North Korean missile crisis, the stack of what we don't know about North Korean missiles would be higher. It's unsettling, but sometimes we just don't know.

Carrie Lam's response to the "five demands" from protestors will not bode well in Hong Kong. She withdrew the controversial bill. The best illustration from Hong Kongers is *a bandaid on a scratch after it turned gangrene.* "Too little, too late" is what most are saying. Expect riots and burning buildings in the weeks to come.

Some Hong Kongers will indeed be satisfied with her speech, dare we say thrilled, but others will be enraged that she waited until after three months and a leaked recording. That recording included Lam's claim that she couldn't resign and that she

had two masters, one of them Beijing. This is
contrary to the autonomy required by the contract
allowing China to claim Hong Kong as its own. If
true, that recording could return Hong Kong to
Britain merely in court. The stakes are high.
Beijing cannot allow the public to believe that the
recording demonstrated any truth. And, apparently
Lam can't either.

If that recording was inaccurate as she said, then
she wouldn't be so angry. Not only did she admit
that the recording was real, it made her angry. Her
objection to it is the recording's greatest notoriety.
But, Confucian Beijing-minded Chinese don't
understand that evidence speaks louder than spin.
They only bake the cake they'll have to lay in.

Withdrawing the bill will be seen by many as an
attempt to counter evidence that Beijing interferes
regularly, violating the Basic Law and the Sino-
British Joint Declaration of 1984. But, the
evidence remains, and there are greater grievances.

Lam's speech fails to address the protests' demand
for her resignation, which is the very subject of the
leaked recording, which came just before her
sudden withdrawal of the bill. The protestors insist
on her resignation and will continue to. When she
said that she never considered resigning, she
further incriminated herself by proving that Hong

Kong does not have its required universal suffrage and that she is part of the reason why.

Some will stop protesting, but those who continue will do so with more veracity. Apart from withdrawing the bill, everything in Lam's video ignores and insults the protest demands, essentially telling the people what they ought to want.

Telling people what they should want is widely accepted in Confucian society. But, it mixes with the West like water with oil. Lam wants to investigate to find out why Hong Kong rejected what are essentially Confucian values. But, there is no disturbance or interference or social trend to investigate. The conflict arose because the Confucian minds controlling Hong Kong, namely Lam and Beijing, are incapable of recognizing that Hong Kong already was Westernized. The question now is whether William Wallace can defeat Mao Tse-Tung.

Encore of Revival: America, September 16

America faces a crossroads. We have enemies mounting against us. Great monsters, fed and allowed to grow, are coming back to haunt us, hunt us, and devour us. It's scary. And, there is a natural tendency to negotiate and avoid provoking wrath of what already wants to eat us.

Some Americans—many, perhaps—have done very bad things in the past. But, many of us learn and improve. Others of us fought against the injustice. Like any nation, America needs to heal, grow, fight the bad, and strengthen the good. We don't need to all lay down and die as our enemies want.

Death comes like a burglar, sneaking in the night. It seeks to isolate, frighten, paralyze first with fear, then with venom, and finally consume. Death makes us long for fear and even death itself. Don't follow its poisonous seduction.

When a people find their heart, no matter how dark times have become, they have what they need to overcome any obstacle. The greatest battle is not over land or law, nor waged with guns or swords, but over the heart and fought with the heart.

We face trying, fearful times. By standing on our values, no matter the cost, we will pay a lesser price in the long run anyway.

Cadence of Conflict: Asia, September 16

China is running into one of the problems of Communism; once the government controls a company, what that company buys is fair game in treaty negotiations. China's government owns a lot of Chinese companies. The world already knows this, but Trump is the first president to figure it out.

Neither Trump nor Xi are attempting any kind of long term trade deal. Xi will only accept a deal where China can grow enough to eradicate the English language from Western culture and the Magna Carta is forgotten, in which case a trade deal wouldn't be necessary anyway. Trump will only accept a trade deal in which that can't happen.

No deal is anticipated by either. Both are vying for time and ways to milk money away from the other to fund their own goals, which are already known, though not everyone has figured them out because not many people want to. We're on a collision course with war and no one wants to admit that.

Delaying the October 1 tariffs because 1. the Chinese premier asked for it and 2. because of the

70th Anniversary celebrating the Chinese Communist Party will only embolden the Chinese Communists. The Chinese love parades, and if they think America respects their parades, they will think it proves that they are invincible. This is a part of Chinese thinking Americans struggle to understand.

Equally, the Chinese struggle to understand Trump. In his Tweet announcement, where he delays the tariffs, but also reminds everyone how bad they will be just two weeks later—it's a mind game that Beijing can't grasp. Even reading this article won't help the Chinese get wise to how much they are being played. The only reason they are so easy to play is because they make it so easy by refusing to abandon their Confucian values. Ironically, those are the very values they want to impose on the rest of the world by Sinicizing the rest of the world.

So, mid-October has become the big date. That's when Trump slaps more tariffs on China, and that's when Taiwan is expected to finalize its purchase of 66 brand-new, shiny, American F-16Vs.

Encore of Revival: America, September 23

Drama, drama, drama... With the celebritization of Kavanaugh, the judiciary is gaining even more power than it had in the past.

The Left is unhappy with new judges who hold the value of "applying the law", rather than judges who "do whatever they think is right". What you think is right might not be what I think is right. Who decides? The law should. Liberals want judges who take sides and create an imbalance. New judges will keep balance and apply the law, even if they disagree with it, thereby giving justice even to their enemies. The only way that the Left hopes to stop this new sweep of justice in our courts is to attack Kavanaugh—but that is only making him famous and, thus, more powerful.

Drama is the Left's way of shooting its foot off. AOC has been a gift to the Republicans. Congressional Democrats just don't get how much they alienate voters with their incessant pushing. Of course there are voters who support their left-of-center ideals, but not most voters. And, they don't know that. And, it's about to cost them the election.

Cadence of Conflict: Asia, September 23

China is dipping into its pork reserves while America is largely unaffected by the surge in oil prices. The pork crisis in China started with an outbreak of the African Swine Flu and has been exacerbated by the trade war. China doesn't have energy independence like America does. Soon, China will have a crisis of both food and energy. Wars have started over less.

Taiwan is ready and on high alert. Though there is a surrender movement in Taiwan as always, Taiwan stands ready with the advantage. Projecting power for an invasion is not as easy as defending an impossible island. With a coastline of either cliffs or marshes and jungle mountains everywhere else, Taiwan is no walk in the park. Taiwan's president is wise to the bullying of China and believes in taking a stand. This is why she supports Hong Kongers as she does.

The situation in Hong Kong is past dire. As foreseen, the protests turned violent because of a deaf government. "No" means "no", but China and its puppets can't bring themselves to accept that, and Hong Kongers won't let "no" mean anything

else. Chinese Confucian Communism now faces
the determination of the West. The great showdown
between the Shame culture of the Far East and the
self-determined culture of the West has begun. It's
only going to escalate. And, all those people who
preached "capitulation to the bully" and the
"invincibility of Chinese Shame" are about to be
proven drastically right or fatefully wrong.

Encore of Revival: America, September 30

The latest assault against Trump for a supposed conspiracy with Ukraine is pure demagoguery fluff. Combining a few scary words in a few scary sentences, attaching the label "whistle blower", then the usual "resistance is futile" Borg propaganda—it wreaks of playbook rehashing. Leftovers chef surprise reheated and re-served might fool dinner guests once or twice. But, triggering alarms that have been often false before won't sway Trump's base for one big reason among many: China.

America faces larger threats than what is being alleged with Ukraine. The accusations aren't alarming to ears that favor Trump. Even if they were serious, Democrats have cried wolf too many times to be taken seriously. If a real scandal actually did hit the presses with Trump, no one who mattered would care. That is the greater danger the Democrats are creating. Just how an award is only as valuable as those who receive it, false alarms make people ignore alarms we shouldn't. We haven't ignored real alarms yet, but

Democrats are laying in the groundwork for it. Maybe that is the real alarm.

Republicans have nothing to lose in playing along because the truth will win in the end anyway. Of course, Democrats mistake Republican "play-along" for Republican "support"—a miscalculation likely to make a Republican 2020 even bigger.

With bigger issues looming, and with the lines blurring between "whistle blower" and "wolf bellower", the American public is more focused on supporting the president who is stopping China from taking over... well, taking over everything. Whoever can stand up to China these days deserves an acquittal, so the voters think, especially an acquittal for doing nothing wrong.

Cadence of Conflict: Asia, September 30

The Hong Kong law currently going through Congress essentially de-escalates, yet therefore intensifies the Hong Kong issue. Rather than prescribing punitive measures if China escalates Hong Kong into military conflict, the law reassesses the unique standing that made Hong Kong so special in the first place. According to these new laws, if China asserts a policy that "Hong Kong is China" too much, then the US will agree and, more or less, remove the diplomatic relationship with Hong Kong. Then, Hong Kong would truly be "China" and no longer valuable to the world.

As for the Human Rights issues, Congress would need no extra law to intervene. The UN and the US already have enough on the books. And, Trump told Xi in no uncertain terms that there would not be a Tienanmen Square Part II.

Through it all, Western globalist fools are being exposed for what fools they are. While Beijing Communists plot the Sinicizaiton of the world, globalists believe that they must keep doing business with China, otherwise their incomes could be cut in half. They never consider that China's goal of growth is not to grow the incomes of globalists, nor to cut incomes in half, but to take all the globalists' money away, then brainwash them into Mandarin-speaking Communists.

For the globalists to rebuke Trump for his trade war would be like telling Moses to continue Israel's slavery in Egypt so that Pharaoh doesn't double their slave-labor workload. The Israeli slaves in Egypt didn't need lighter slave work loads; they needed freedom. Some globalists still haven't figured that out, but they will, thanks to China.

But, none of that will matter inside China, not this week anyway. Tomorrow, the Chinese will look at evidence of their perfection and greatness—a specific kind of evidence that persuades the Chinese more than anything else. In the midst of protests and trade wars, China is having a parade; and that is why China wants you to believe China should rule the world.

Encore of Revival: America, October 7

President Trump has been a role model for America's place in the world: non-interference. Fighting revolutionary wars for others is a bad idea. It has only backfired. Pakistan, Afghanistan, and Iraq are just a few examples. Hong Kong's October 4 declaration of a provisional government is a model of what should be done to help another democratic revolution: nothing. Real democratic revolutions must happen on their own and Trump knows that. He might be the only president in our time to know that.

Even though he does not interfere as presidents before him have, the non-interference fans among Democrats continue to attack him. That, too, is backfiring.

The president has an obligation to investigate criminals. Joe Biden and his son have extremely dubious financial entanglements and possible connection to elements Robert Mueller investigated. If the Mueller investigation was so important, then President Trump ought to pursue loose ends that Mueller and Congressional Democrats didn't. When a foreign country is party to elements of such a serious investigation as Mueller's, as well as extremely dubious dealings of the Bidens, the Attorney General of the United States ought to cooperate with the government of that country through official channels.

Trump asked for just that and no more.

Trump did not ask to connect secret attorneys or organizations. He did not request back door channels. He did not ask for unofficial cooperation. And, the people he wanted to investigate were not without serious suspicions.

Had President Trump not asked Ukrainian President Zelensky for the official cooperation he did, Trump would not have been doing his job as president. As for Biden and the supposed "political campaign rivals" accusation Congressional Democrats conjured, Joe Biden should be aware that running for president doesn't allow a candidate to break the law without being investigated. Biden started his dubious dealings long before he was a presidential hopeful. If claiming "for political purposes" is granted to every candidate under investigation, Democrats could make crime vanish merely by declaring the entire population to be political candidates.

Cadence of Conflict: Asia, October 7

Hong Kong has declared independence! On Friday, October 4, thousands peacefully gathered in Ma On Shan at New Hong Kong City Centre and read aloud a manifesto. This manifesto included basic arguments similar to the US Declaration of Independence, along with basic steps for a provisional government until the new government takes over. In the eyes of China, this will be treason, just as the US Declaration of Independence was treason in the eyes of Britain.

There has been no bigger news in almost 200 years. No nation has stood up to a world superpower so great since the American Colonies defied the world-dominating British Empire in 1776. Suspiciously, mainstream news agencies were utterly silent about this all weekend.

The next question is whether Hong Kong will be able to resist China's military. That question can only be answered by historians who have studied asymmetric warfare, such as the First War of Scottish Independence in 1270, the American Revolutionary War of 1775, or Vietnam's August Revolution of 1945.

Britain would be wise to help because that might allow the Crown to hold Hong Kong among the Commonwealth afterward. The UN is calling for an investigation into how China has handled the four months of protest, so it would seem that the world is on Hong Kong's side. But, investigations always follow long after a crime, even against Human Rights, while the people are left to defend themselves until help arrives. Can Hong Kong join the successful revolutionaries of history?

The string of anti-extradition protests began March 31, this year, 190 days ago. The protests have been in a state of ongoing outbreak since June 9. Hong Kongers have lived and fought in unrest in their own home for 120 days straight. They have overpowered a 32,000 troupe police force the entire time. Hong Kongers have thus become formidable and battle-tested with inferior weaponry. The impossible odds—fighting with bamboo sticks against guns—make the typical Jackie Chan movie prophetic. If China's PLA soldiers think they will have an easy time suppressing Hong Kong, they have news in store. It's not impossible. Only history will tell.

Unrest turned to turmoil on October 2, when China held its 70th Anniversary parade for the Communist Party. America will soon join Hong Kong's objection to China in its own way.

In Beijing, showing off the old-news, well-known DF-41 hypersonic, "can-hit-America-in-30-minutes" 10-nuke-warhead missiles was a miscalculation. America is not afraid because we don't expose the limits of our tech in parades. Most of our most-advanced military tech isn't known to the general public, which is somewhat how the American people want it to be, kind of. Seeing this flagrant, open threat will motivate the inventors and businesses in the wealthier, higher-tech America to neutralize China's open threats ASAP. Some are calling it a "Sputnik moment".

China is a nation that thinks itself to be stronger than it actually is. If it rises to even a quarter of the world domination it hopes, it would be the first time a superpower rose from a nation so ancient. Since Persia, all world superpowers of history rose from new nations built on the encouragement of new ideas, legal limits of government, and rights for citizens. China is not on a quest to defy the world; it is on a quest to defy history. Hong Kong has history on its side.

Encore of Revival: America, October 14

Who does Pat Roberson think he is? Who gets to say whether or what America's "mandate from Heaven" is? We can talk about Kurds and allies and defending the defenseless. But, once we start using grandiose terms like "Heaven's mandate", that opens a whole new discussion.

If we're going to go all Bible-thumping Bible-happy about America and Heaven, we need to look at what John saw in Heaven in Revelation 12, where a woman and her newborn baby are given eagle's wings and saved from a dragon. The woman giving birth is Israel. The eagle's wings could only be America. If anyone is going to argue that America even has a mandate from Heaven—which may or may not be true—it would be to protect 1. Israel and 2. the unborn. But, that's assuming that America even has such a mandate. Syria, as much as we all should love all people, is not part of Revelation 12 and should be left out of this melodramatic "mandate from Heaven" freak talk.

Yes, America—and every other country—should all look after human rights and the good of *all people* —not only Christians, but non-Christians as well.

Pat Robertson presumes the old, classic, "us four and no more" thinking we have come to sadly expect from Sunday morning culture. As for Syria, Russia is there and should be able to police wild stuff. America is spread too thin. And, the world would be safer if more nations hunkered down and stayed home. Scary and unpopular as it sounds, America needs to pull out of Syria because we don't have the unlimited resources of God and because we are indeed needed elsewhere.

Who should look after the Christians in Syria? The Christians should. Rather than playing on old superstitions, such as that America exists to favor Christians or that "good Christians" squabble over petty differences, Christians should act like the family they are. Jesus told Peter, "Those who live by the sword die by the sword." Military might is not how God works with Christians. He uses military to direct global politics, but shooting enemies of the Sunday crowd is not God's mode of operation, no matter how much Mr. Robertson thinks so. Heaven cares about Christians, but its strategy for Christians is to love each other and spread love— that is Heaven's mandate for how Christians should be looked after.

When we face our challenges, some leaders cower in fear, too scared to give an answer that should seem obvious. When asked the trap-question,

"Should the president ask a foreign government to investigate a political rival?" the obvious answer is, "If the rival broke the laws of that government, of course! Otherwise no Republican or Democrat would be able to enforce laws against the other." Why can't Republicans say that? When one finds oneself with power one didn't earn, one won't know how to beat the toughest problems, no matter how obvious things may seem to everyone else. Congressional Republicans will either level-up their game or pack up and go home. This isn't pee-wee politics anymore.

Democrats in Congress seem to have forgotten all about looking after Americans, though. The House is trying to impeach a president who won't be removed by the Senate—it's pointless. But, to understand Democrats, one must understand the Democratic voters. They might not know that impeachment is pointless, just how Mr. Robertson doesn't know that a "mandate from Heaven" comes from Heaven, not sensationalist TV. But, sensationalism is the trend, for now.

Cadence of Conflict: Asia, October 14

You can't bring a pot to boil forever. While the conventional narrative for Hong Kong warns, "Retribution is coming," a better understanding would be, "The Chinese are coming if Hong Kong doesn't level up." The protests must either "level up" or otherwise change, or else the PLA will indeed march and smash.

While the situation in Hong Kong is deteriorating into a cultural war—a defense against an invasive culture of Sinicization—talks between the US and China took a similar cultural detour for the worst. China doesn't want so-called "interference" with kidnapping 1.5 million Muslims in Xinjiang, in Beijing's view "internal matters". By that definition, "internal matters" violate international Human Rights laws.

Trump's words, that all is well in Hong Kong, elude Hong Kongers and Chinese as much as the American media. On the surface Trump appeared to praise the doctored press reports coming out of Hong Kong. He also praised Supreme Justice Kavanaugh's accuser, Christine Ford, days before mocking her. Not one main news agency reported

Hong Kong's October 4 de facto declaration of independence with plans for rebellion elections. Praising evidentially censored reports from Hong Kong surmounts to little.

Still, Trump knows the ramifications of his words. By playing along with propaganda China would normally get resistance from, and by staying hands-off, Trump was indirectly telling Beijing that he knows Hong Kong is worse than reported while also letting Hong Kong learn the hard lesson that independence starts with expecting no help from the outside. Over the weekend we saw just that, including smaller flash-protests and perching the Hong Kong "Goddess of Democracy" atop Lion Rock in Kowloon. "Careless Carrie" Lam even cancelled a meeting with Senator Ted Cruz—after his 10+ hour overnight flight landed.

Trump's words could lead to the very "level-up" game-changer the Hong Kong protesters must make in order to survive. One should guess that Trump doesn't want Hong Kong to "just be okay", but to earn whatever independence they get on their own. It feels like rejection at first, but being abandoned to earn one's own victory—and the spoils with it—is the greater gift of a friend. Trump never said he would squash Hong Kongers' call for independence; he simply refused to steal their thunder.

The Chinese probably won't pick up on Trump's subtlety because Confucianism—especially Communist Confucianism—doesn't believe anything can happen without outside "help". This is the only reason Beijing suspects supposed "Western interference" without a shred of evidence.

So, the trade agreement seems to be okay, this week. But, China doesn't want to be told to let its economy play by the same rules as ours because that too is "internal". There is one key flaw with China's thinking: entitlement.

Of course, America should not dictate what type of economy is best for China or any other nation. At the same time, trade is a privilege not a right. By America requiring a free market as a condition for trade with another free market, America is not interfering, but refusing to be interfered with.

Just the same, Beijing claims to reject a "zero-sum game" deal. What they mean is that they want a zero-sum game in China's favor because they believe being better than everyone else is their right. If America doesn't lose so that China can gain, China will reject the deal as unfair, just as they did with Britain in the "silver-for-leaves" trade that led to the Opium Wars. Nothing has changed.

The virtue of compromise doesn't work in dealing with China, whether as an American trade negotiator or as a citizen of Hong Kong. When China demands 100, then we compromise at 50, China will demand another 100 again tomorrow. If we compromise again, it would be 100-0, and it would happen all over again the next day and the next. China will keep demanding to expand and overrun everyone else. By China's China-favoring standards, the only compromise stands on how fast China takes you over, either ultra fast or slowly. For Beijing, there is no room for the words in the Book of Job where God told the ocean, "Here, and no farther."

Encore of Revival: America, October 21

Trump is set to redefine historical trends. Every thumbscrew play from the political playbook has been tried on him and every single one has failed except the impeachment in progress, which hasn't failed or succeeded yet. The very impeachment process will only boost his support as already seen in Texas. It's all based on results.

Trump supporters and Conservatives—not necessarily one in the same—respond to and respond with results.

Divisions are solidifying along every line—religion, politics, social justice wars. Two people with opposing views can't reason with each other. Those on the Conservative side tend to be quiet and work and vote. Those on the Liberal side are loud and make anyone who dissents regret it.

The more these divisions and assaults build, the more we see rhetoric face off against results. Loud Liberals in America think they identify with the protesters in Hong Kong. But, it's not being outspoken that makes a protest work, it's the resolve to be left alone.

Many Conservatives would be glad to lift laws that make life difficult for the LGBTQ community. But, the social justice war now seeks to punish people for pronouns. That social justice war will likely lead to a backlash from the Conservatives who could eventually place more restrictions on the LGBTQ community than ever before. Overplaying is a danger for everyone. But, no one can be reasoned with these days.

With Senator Romney pushing against the president in his own party, a president popular among Conservatives and many Democrats, he could be paving the way for a third party two presidents after Trump.

Cadence of Conflict: Asia, October 21

"Careless" Carrie Lam's effectiveness in Hong Kong is in the red. After banning masks at public gatherings, more people are wearing masks at gatherings than in the past. She bans an assembly, but people assemble anyway. Protests are so bad, police hit some people guarding a mosque with a water cannon and had to apologize to the imam. Lam was heckled by legislators during her annual policy speech and had to leave the chamber twice, finally delivering her speech on television. A government so defied and can't govern. But, the need for public trust isn't understood by Confucianism nor Communism nor especially Confucian Communism.

Beyond loss of control, the West gets the message loud and clear: China won't back down on its forced expansionism. US Congress continues to pass laws favoring freedom in both Hong Kong and Taiwan. The TAIPEI act is largely symbolic, but still meaningful inasmuch as it gauges China's response. Evaluating Hong Kong's level of autonomy to be treated as a separate territory from China makes sense. Still, China considers the US formulating its own international policy a form of "interference". Think about that...

US international policy must be what China wants it to be, otherwise China labels this as "interference". This can only mean that China considers the US already under Chinese rule. It's no longer about whether or to what extent China can boss Hong Kong and Taiwan. Now, the question is whether China should be allowed to dictate another country's foreign policy.

Another factor is corporate. Gaming companies oust gamers who make "political" statements to defend freedom and human rights, but then Dior gets political by apologizing to China for not putting Taiwan in its map of China. If companies were consistent about being so-called "non-political", then Dior would have refused to agree or disagree with China. But, this isn't about being non-political; it's about agreeing with whatever China demands.

Encore of Revival: America, October 28

People must rise up for freedom on their own. Protestors in Hong Kong have stood up for their own freedom; the same should be expected of the Kurds in Syria. If they face persecution, offer asylum or refugee status. There could be a political solution or a referendum that must be honored, like the referendum in Crimea. But, don't fight someone else's freedom war for them. Freedom cannot be bestowed, only fought for and defended by the freed folk themselves.

Democrats seeking impeachment without a vote first sets a precedent for Republicans to more easily oust a Democratic president in the future. Many Democrat-driven laws initially meant to curb Republicans came back to bite Democrats when it was their turn to follow their own new laws. A no-vote impeachment proceeding could also impede Congressional ability to enforce subpoenas against another branch of government or to continue to hold hearings in the basement SCIF.

America faces a Constitutional crisis on two fronts: first, impeachment, subpoenas, no official impeachment vote, and whether a Supreme Justice who offered political comments about the President can preside over a trial in the Senate; second, California's legal authority to enter into an international treaty apart from the Federal Government. By joining the "carbon credits" cult with Canada, California engaged in the kind of international negotiations that the Constitution explicitly prohibits in Article II Section 2 Clause 2, which made the Constitution different from its predecessor, the Articles of Confederation. While California focused on the environment more than the Constitution, it left kindling unattended throughout forests now on fire. Trump warned about the uncollected kindling wood and leaves in the forests of California over one year ago and is suing California for its carbon credit agreement with Canada.

We are in conflict. The nation is in conflict. There are two Americas today, just as there were two types of Pilgrims aboard the Mayflower. The battle in our divided nation rages hotter than California's fires. Stewardship of the economy, national security, and the environment can all play well with rule of law. Whoever understands that the best will come out ahead in this great American conflict.

Cadence of Conflict: Asia, October 28

China is playing a dark game with Taiwan over the murder suspect in the case that sparked the spark of the Hong Kong liberation protests. A young man from Hong Kong traveled to Taiwan with his girlfriend where he murdered her, then returned to Hong Kong. Because China plays politics with Taiwan, Beijing refused every channel of cooperation with Taipei to bring the suspect to justice. The only way Beijing would allow the arrested suspect to be transferred to Taiwan for prosecution is with a sweeping extradition bill that would allow any Chinese court to demand the extradition of anyone in Hong Kong to China.

Now, Hong Kong has released the suspect, arguing that a criminal is on the loose in Hong Kong because Taiwan won't accept Chinese dictated rule.

We are witnessing the faceoff of Chinese Confucianism vs Western Christendom, a conflict which has been brewing for two thousand years. This is happening in our day. Many in the West said that Confucian Shame cannot be overcome, even with the Christian message of forgiveness and reconciliation. Others have said that nothing can ever stop China because big countries always win. All of these claims are about to be tested and proven wrong. Hard times lie ahead, but not all hardship ends badly.

Encore of Revival: America, November 4

American conflicts are hitting the fan, just like the fake trade war with China. Democratic-run cities, like Chicago and New York, face high debt and high crime rates piled up like a mountain of garbage over so many years. Trump said so, garnering support from his base and harnessing rage from his opposition. Blowback from Democrats over his anti-Democrat comments will help his poll numbers, just how anti-Republican comments from a Democratic candidate do.

While some in the Republican establishment still think that acting like a Republican will repel Republican voters, an ever-apparently, ever-larger quiet majority of Conservative-minded voters are quietly standing up to prove quite tall. People are fed up with algorithms making social media recommendations and are shopping elsewhere. Conservative voices are letting Liberal subscribers walk out the door.

LGBTQ does have more rights than before Obama, but no longer in every adoption case, according to a new Trump rule. No one should get the run of the farm, Conservative or Liberal. Gridlock keeps honest people honest.

The impeachment campaign against Trump will help him in the end. Eventually, if it continues, the Republican minority will be allowed to question the Bidens. The Democratic base will then strengthen, and many independent voters will switch to the Republican ticket for the 2020 election, granting Republicans a gain in the Senate and control of the House. As good as that might sound for Republican voters, nothing is as dangerous as a supermajority, no matter who it is. Fortunately, that's still not the end.

Cadence of Conflict: Asia, November 4

The crud is hitting the fan on China and the fake trade war. The US and China were ready to sign, until they weren't. They were going to sign at APEC in Chile, but Chilean society's peace seems to be mirroring that of Hong Kong. Protests seem to be getting in the way of many things related to China.

While a small part of a trade deal might be signed between the US and China, the World Trade Organization approved Chinese sanctions against the US to the tune of $3.6B USD. The ruling was based on things like "zeroing" and "anti-dumping". Basically, the WTO thinks it's fair for Chinese factories to sell a product in China for $50, then sell the same product in America for $25 to get a monopoly in America. The US government doesn't agree.

Hong Kong protests are worse all around. "About 200" people were arrested just this past weekend. One Mandarin-speaking pro-Beijinger started knifing people, then bit off a man's ear before being arrested. China's solution to the protests about Chinese intervention is to intervene more and to "improve" the non-autonomy methods of Hong

Kong, which was supposed to have autonomy and still doesn't. Hong Kong CEO Carrie Lam envisions a new Hong Kong that the world will trust and love, based on Chinese intervention and strict law enforcement everywhere.

Taiwan gains more international sympathy. The US is introducing yet another law, more or less aimed at stepping-up Taiwan's presence on the world stage—while at the same time seeking to resolve a disagreement that purportedly started over trade.

Encore of Revival: America, November 11

Scandal after scandal, controversy after controversy—America is divided over ideas. For many, their solution is to talk, argue, theorize, analyze, and strategize. While their constant clucking reaches ears outside the hen house, other people in Washington are actually doing something.

The DOJ is pursuing a genuine criminal investigation of the FBI's role with what has become the Russianewsgategate scandal. It started with an accusation about Russia based on the news rather than evidence, then they tried to make it into a scandal, then the fake scandal became a scandal. Now, Comey and Brennan could be looking at jail time, even treason, in an attempted coup.

Typically, Washington Congressional hearings carry clout and intimidation. The political puppets line up around the room on an elevated bench and look down on the witness giving testimony. Behind the witness is a packed crowd with standing room only. That's how confirmation hearings and impeachment hearings and other televised hearings go. That was ENRON, General Motors, Condi Rice, Olly North, Brett Kavanaugh, Clarence Thomas, even John Kerry's testimony about Vietnam before he was a Senator. It's scary, even spooky, but that's about it.

Lights, camera, action! Congressional hearings are a show designed to stir the pot of voters. As Americans grow bored with the news, Congressional theater is losing whatever power it might have wielded. So, while the actors, performers, and thespians give their show on Capitol Hill, the DOJ is actually doing something substantive. Attorney General William Barr isn't putting on any kind of show trial. This is serious. And, it's moving forward at the speed of law. And, perhaps for the first time, the usual performers will need to lawyer-up.

It doesn't matter so much what people say; it matters what people do. America is divided over ideas. The biggest source of division is whether to perform or whether to actually do something real. Another performance will probably be their defense.

Cadence of Conflict: Asia, November 11

Hong Kong has presented the world with the ethical question of confronting bullies. Say there is a bully at school who quietly eats whosever lunch he wants, stealing anyone's homework he wants, until one day someone says something and the bully gets violent. In theory, most people agree that the bully started it. But in practice, when it comes time to stand up to the bullies of life, even the biggest Braveheart fans place the blame for the fight on the one who had the conscience to stand up to the bully. So, are Hong Kong protestors to blame for not going along to get along while China quietly violates its treaty with the UK, denies human rights, and refuses to regulate police conduct?

China says restoring social order in Hong Kong is the "most pressing issue", but obviously not as important as destroying anything that stands in the way of Chinese Communist hegemony.

In a double-standard, Taiwan is having to adjust its laws to deal with Chinese interference. The CCP is paying news outlets to spread its propaganda in Taiwan. It got caught having a fake news site and is now resorting to outsourcing. The Taiwanese don't think that publishing what China tells someone to publish is "free speech".

Xi Jinping's decision to keep Carrie Lam as CEO of Hong Kong only makes sense, notwithstanding it proves interference by pure definition. The Chinese Communist Party would never dispose of such an efficient creator of chaos. Chaos is always the first phase of the CCP taking over a resistant people; the second phase is to send in the military and—well, do what China's military does so well. While the Western press explains keeping Carrie as a way to avoid opening a can of worms, the Chinese have much more sinister intentions as history proves.

More crud hit the fan this week, over and over, again and again, evermore. A college student not connected with a nearby protest tried to escape a parking lot just after police fired tear gas, then fell to his death. As expected, police denied any wrongdoing.

A woman rumored to be only 16 years old passed a police station Tsuen Wan where she claims to have been ordered inside, then gang raped by four masked men. Meeting some of the criteria of a rape victim, she found she was pregnant a few weeks after the incident, the young woman was reportedly suffering from depression, and had an abortion last Thursday. The investigation is ongoing, but, in the current atmosphere, police have done little elsewhere to stop such stories from being believable.

Over the weekend, police arrested six lawmakers who effectively filibustered Carrie Lam's annual report back in May. Six reporters wore Chinese letters on hardhats at a police press conference, spelling a Cantonese request to investigate police. This was in response to two reporters having been arrested. The police department sent formal objection letters to the six reporters' press agencies. Lawmakers and journalists should be immune to such arrests in order to prevent political interference. But, Hong Kong police no longer wear ID tags on their uniforms, and China says the unrest in Hong Kong started because police don't have enough power.

Western foreigners visiting Hong Kong have started to join protests. It's arguably bad form, though it indicates that the world feels a sense of solidarity in standing up to China's bullying anywhere and everywhere it happens. China sees it as proof of interference while the West sees it as successful marketing from the Hong Kong protesters. The problem with China's "interference proof" argument is that foreign attendees after the fact do not prove any causality before the fact. But, when being a mouthpiece rather than a think tank has been the habit for so long, Chinese wouldn't understand the difference.

Encore of Revival: America, November 18

The trade war with China has hurt American farmers—just as a year of bad weather also hurt American farmers. Notwithstanding questions of why Americans chose to become dependent on Communists as their customer, the larger culprit should be large corporations competing against small farmers, seeking a de facto monopoly. Bigness is set against the small guy in America. Trump's trade war sees the biggest competitor of any American business as the Chinese Communist government itself—since the Chinese government financially supports companies competing against non-government companies in America.

This is a recipe for war. Rather than hating Trump, farmers will blame the Chinese and support the coming war that the fake trade war was meant to lead up to all along. Secretary of State Pompeo certainly is ready.

Few things re-elect presidents like a widely-supported war. Washington Democrats are not playing to win the next election; they are playing for employment. They know that they can't win the presidency or the Senate in 2020 and will most likely lose the House. Everything they have done in 2019, and are continuing to do through this next election, is designed to keep their voters preoccupied and distracted from the approaching failure.

If the Democratic electorate stays singularly focused on victories that will never happen, then enough of them will go to the polls to keep the majority of current Democrats in Washington employed, but Democrats will no longer be the majority in Washington. The entire assault against Trump is a shear distraction, designed by Democratic politicians to dupe their own base into marching toward utter failure so they can keep some of their seats on Capitol Hill.

The most recent episode of Russianewsgategate is a glaring example. Marie Yovanovitch, an Obama-appointed ambassador, was working as if still for Obama even though Trump was president. The Ukraine president didn't like it. She was rightfully fired. Disgruntled, now it's her moment of payback —as a witness in matters she had nothing to do with. The House hearings on Trump are a mere show trial. Don't expect the electorate to respond any differently—those who enjoy the show will keep their plans to vote against Trump and those who don't like the show will vote for him.

Cadence of Conflict: Asia, November 18

America and China are getting fed up with China and America being fed up with each other. Americans tried patience and negotiations; that didn't work. China hid its agenda for global domination, denouncing so-called "interference" except when China did the interfering. Now, China's true colors are showing and it looks like a lot of debt. Municipalities and local governments are buried in debt, which is eating at China's central economy like Asian ants on a morning worm.

Amid riots and threats, encroachments by police on university campuses and by China upon Hong Kong rule, the primary issue in Hong Kong is the upcoming revolution election in March. On October 4, Hong Kongers declared the current government already nullified and that interim government elections would take place in March. That election is not the primary concern for most reports coming out of Hong Kong, if it gets mentioned at all. But, that election should be the primary concern of China, the United States, and the current—and denounced—Hong Kong government. Perhaps those upcoming elections have not been taken seriously, and, if so, that would be perhaps the most serious miscalculation.

But, rather than carefully calculating the right way forward, China is more concerned with optics—not with causing good optics, but with countering bad optics with more mere optics.

The same Plague from the Black Death has re-emerged in China's Inner Mongolia province. Historically, whether in 541, 1347, or 1894, the Plague always had its origins in the Far East. Rather than promptly confronting the source, the Chinese are basically doing what the San Francisco government did in the early 1900s: covering it up.

Even Chinese soldiers play the optics game. Chinese Communist PLA soldiers are not allowed to leave their garrisons in Hong Kong without a formal request from Hong Kong's government. But, they did anyway—to clear streets blocked by protestors. They didn't clash with protestors, they simply picked up stuff in the street, mostly bricks. They weren't armed nor did they wear fatigues; they wore running shorts and OD-green T-shirts, the same that they exercise in on a daily basis. But, they weren't invited by the Hong Kong government. As a result, their presence was technically illegal, though seemingly helpful in the minds of some residents who want to drive down the street.

Interestingly, the unarmed, seemingly-harmless soldiers were accompanied by cameras; it was a publicity stunt. Voices in the British Commonwealth are especially concerned because this beautiful, warm, kindhearted photo-op sets a precedent of PLA soldiers breaching Hong Kong illegally. Chinese thinking puts logic before law, which feels like justice at first, but then operates with no standard of conduct, deciding right and wrong from one moment to the next. In other words, Beijing thinks that China's soldiers must not enter Hong Kong uninvited—unless they want to.

Encore of Revival: America, November 25

Calling on a foreign government to investigate its own dubious dealings with dubious Americans isn't criminal. Not all political rivalries are trivial. The Bidens should be the political enemy of anyone honest. Trump should be praised for his call to the Ukraine, not impeached. But, it looks like impeachment is where the Democratic train is headed and there is no getting off.

Formally impeaching the president will irritate the American public into voting even more Republican in the next election than already was going to happen. And, it will give subpoena power to Republicans in the Senate. Somehow, Democrats in Washington think that is a victory. But, then Democrats and their most loyal voters have always evaluated by methods rather than results. We shouldn't expect that to change. No matter how much the results hurt, Leftist thinking is generally numb to results.

While the impeachment saga trudges on toward a Republican supermajority, the DOJ continues to pursue criminal charges against the

Russianewsgategate coup attempt of 2016. Eventually, that could implicate Schiff.

The world faces a transformative crisis. From defecting Chinese Communists to Hong Kong's autonomy to Taiwan's independence to US impeachment, all the way to Brexit—nations are soul-searching and wrestling with their demons. This is not any result of political "strategery"; it is the result of a praying Church. That worldwide, unofficial Church will only continue to grow and pray more transformation into being.

Cadence of Conflict: Asia, November 25

Hong Kong's election results from yesterday have confirmed the general public's view: Hong Kongers reject China's actions. Not that it will make a difference—elected officials don't hold a majority in Hong Kong's legislative process. But, pro-Beijing officials were voted-out, replaced with pro-democracy candidates who campaigned on "5-demands". There had been speculation as to how much Hong Kongers supported the "5-demand" protests; this morning there is no doubt. Taiwan, the US, and the UK generally oppose the manner of Chinese expansion; this morning we know Hong Kong does too.

It was always easy to see why.

When the US Senate unanimously passed its own version of a bill that would annually evaluate whether Hong Kong was autonomous enough for it to be treated autonomously, China went berserk and accused the US of interfering. When Hong Kong's High Court overturned Hong Kong's recent ban on masks, Beijing rebuked the court, thereby proving that Beijing believes Hong Kong is not a separate jurisdiction from the rest of China.

Apparently, Beijing thinks Hong Kong should have its government utterly determined by Beijing, but should be treated as if the opposite were true. In America we call this "wanting to have your cake and eat it too"; in China it's called "Communism".

US Congress has sweeping bipartisan agreement to determine what the US does in its foreign relations. The US decides whether to sell riot gear to another country. China calls this "interference"; in America that's called "blame-shifting". Albeit, China has been illegally interfering in Hong Kong, Taiwan, and even working to undermine Australia's government, according to a Chinese Communist spy who recently defected Down Under. $200M USD to thwart Taiwan's election—and China thinks the US is meddling by not selling rubber bullets to Hong Kong police. It's no wonder yesterday's election turned out as it did.

Several students holed up in Polytechnic University in Hung Hom tried to walk out, but police chased them back in with tear gas—purportedly because they wanted the students to leave. That was a few days before the US Senate passed its bill about Hong Kong's autonomy being defined by autonomy. While the intentions of the police seem to be contradictory, there is a greater danger Hong Kong's government is blind to.

While under siege and later trying to escape, the students and countless new protestors who joined the cause because of the police response, have learned new skills. They are gaining practice at launching Molotov cocktails, shooting police officers with old fashion archery, rappelling in free air, organizing supply and movement lines, along with other aspects of urban guerilla resistance that neither Hong Kong's police nor China's PLA are trained for. Carrie Lam has turned these now three plus million protestors into one of the most formidable military forces in Asia, if not the most per capita.

A civilian military is necessary for any nation's independence. Before these protests, Hong Kong never met that unwritten-yet-real requirement. Since Carrie Lam made the decisions that she did, now Hong Kong has a different truth. As relevant and telling as yesterday's election was, the more important election is coming in March, when Hong Kong's October 4 Declaration of Independence scheduled its provisional election. With a now-experienced civilian militia, Hong Kong has all the pieces it needs for a successful revolution. That should not be ignored, but it is.

Encore of Revival: America, December 2

"Order in the ranks" of military discipline includes that the president is the commander in chief who always gets his way—in the military. Generals and secretaries in the US Armed Forces have zero preference in any disagreement of decision with the president. As commander in chief, the president can overturn any court-martial conviction and fire or dismiss anyone for any reason. This is intended by the Constitution so that the Armed Forces serve the will of the people. The military does not give orders to the democratically elected president. Anyone in the Armed Forces attempting to circumvent a decision of the president should be discharged and possibly prosecuted for mutiny— based on Article 94 (§ 894)(a)(1) of the 2004 *Uniform Code of Military Justice* definition of Mutiny or Sedition. It is inappropriate for anyone to claim fowl play in the the Navy secretary's firing.

Kevin Clinesmith from the FBI has been dubbed the title "frontline lawyer". He reportedly doctored evidence in the FISA spy application as part of the Russianewsgategate scandal. If he was not acting under the explicit direction of his "behind the frontlines" superiors, then the Obama administration's FBI, including James Comey, had even bigger problems. "Frontline lawyers" at the FBI are supposed to follow instructions of the director, otherwise the director is AWOL.

As impeachment moves forward, Democrats seal their fate. They've already gone too far. Whether the House votes to impeach, Democrats lose popularity. Either they let down their base or they anger everyone Right of staunch Democratic voters with unnecessary drama. Two unanswered questions remain: Will they choose to lose votes by impeaching or lose votes by not impeaching? And, more mysteriously, are they secretly trying to help President Trump or are have they been operating on kook-directed autopilot so long that they are no longer capable of knowing where they are headed?

The biggest danger Donald Trump always posed was that he would do too well and thus give Republicans a supermajority they couldn't have earned on their own. No one seems to be helping that effort as much as House Democrats. Fortunately for the country, the ever-less-so silent majority doesn't make political decisions on autopilot. And, that majority is growing larger.

Cadence of Conflict: Asia, December 2

Opinions on Asia aren't just flying, but swarming the Pacific. Hong Kongers vote against China in an unmistakable slap to Beijing's face, then Beijing blames the US—because Beijing still thinks that voters only vote how the government tells them to. And, everything is all America's fault anyway, right?

It took a day of silence for Beijing's media machine to figure out how to spin the election. Beijing accused Hong Kong's dissent on violence. But, that doesn't hold since last week's election went uninterrupted. Yet, Beijing sticks to the same script.

A commentator predicts that Hong Kongers don't want independence—even though they already declared independence on October 4. Perhaps Doris Lam's article on Channel News Asia was an attempt to tell Hong Kongers what they should want. Or, it could have been an attempt to tell Beijing to think that Hong Kongers don't want what they want. Either way, it is a delusional olive branch in the form of a typical long-worded think piece. There is a growing trend of commentators who make their articles longer when they know that few readers will accept their opinions.

After Trump signs two laws about Hong Kong—one to define an autonomous region as autonomous, the other to stop exporting police tools for riot-control—Beijing calls it "interference". Then, Trump drops tariffs on China because good ole Benjamin is hard to argue with. Yet, Beijing wants more. Now, as in Chinese business negotiation, China wants to change the deal after everything has been agreed to. They want even lower tariffs in Phase One.

Great Britain wants UN access to Xinjiang. China wants the world to believe Xinjiang is happy, an Islamic utopia; new documents prove otherwise. China also faces a food shortage, but a good marketing effort is underway for investment in Chinese farming. Stopping any possible abuse of Uyghurs in Xinjiang is interference in Beijing's opinion, but accepting foreign money to build better farms isn't. Perhaps Beijing will call it interference if the rest of the world *does not* invest in Chinese farms.

Taiwan's election is fast approaching. Though Tsai Ing-Wen, the pro-democracy incumbent president, leads in the polls, many Taiwanese are scared that there are too many voters in the old, beaten-down generation for her to win a second time. Older Taiwanese, like many Chinese, have been so dominated by East Asia's shame culture that they truly believe that "bigness" always wins and therefore they must vote for politicians who will surrender to China. Younger Taiwanese have seen this older generation get its way so many times, even polls can't keep them from being scared. But, as John Maynard Keynes said, "Men will not always die quietly." Few things drive voters to the polls like fear of dying at the hands of politicians who want to surrender. Tsai Ing-Wen is set to win by an even greater margin than she did in her first term—and everyone has something to say about it.

Encore of Revival: America, December 9

This week, we caught a closer glimpse of what the impeachment hearings in the House are truly about: election 2020. Democrats can't win and they know it. This impeachment is their best chance to lose less of the vote, but it may backfire.

The reason opposition news against Trump doesn't sway his base is because of what it reveals about actual, normal life. Usually, the president and Congress are portrayed as operating "above" everyone else, never having any problems, or at least that they only have problems that us normal people never have. But, every accusation and difference of opinion reported about Trump reveals that every president—not just he—deals with the same, constant, nonsensical heckling from people at the office that all the rest of us deal with.

Some friends always act like they have a better idea when they actually haven't a clue. Doing the only thing that can save a company or school always makes people mad—especially if those are the very people who drove problems to the brink of crisis. As movers and shakers shake and move to save the world from idiots who shouldn't have been put in charge, those idiots refuse to give us a moment's peace, even when they are close friends and family.

So, you see, Trump deals with the same kind of nonsense that every competent person deals with. We just didn't know until his adversaries told us so —as if we hadn't already seen it before.

Cadence of Conflict:
Asia, December 9

Money doesn't lie; it's in the airline figures. Cathay is reducing its capacity, largely from loss of demand for flights in and out of China. Hong Kong Airlines is dropping long hauls to and from Australia, the US, and Canada. Clearly, both Chinese nationals and Pacific English speakers have lost confidence in Hong Kong. Hong Kong was special—for tourism, culture, lifestyle, trade, finance, and a slough of other things—all because both Chinese and the English-speaking West had easy and overlapping access. They could meet, they could do business, they could speak their own language, and they could enjoy Chinese culture without the oppression of a Confucian-Communist government. But, neither wants to play ball anymore.

In response to the US ending exports of riot-control weapons and defining autonomy as "being autonomous", China banned the US Navy from making port stops in Hong Kong. The port stops had been an encouragement to international business, reassuring investors that everything was alright between the US and China. But, apparently

China doesn't want that illusion of reassurance to continue. And, more importantly, China obviously is less fearful of the US Navy making its R&R port calls in Taiwan instead.

Watch for many things to shift to Taiwan. While the first finance leaders in Hong Kong are exiting to Singapore, watch for a swath to relocate in Taipei once Singapore's galore wears off and finance centers discover the difference in real estate prices and cost of living.

China will still be angry enough to blow a few gaskets when the US Navy does make more port calls in Taiwan, it's just that they are less fearful of it for the time being. China's leaders have been had, largely due to their thirst for respect, which blinds their judgement. But, they are incapable of learning, so they are only going to be had more and more.

Encore of Revival: America, December 16

Revelations about the Russianewsgategate scandal are beyond damning. Why would Comey and friends consciously fabricate a lie, just to scare the president for not meeting with the Intelligence community every day? Generally, the public thinks that they think that their attempted assault against the president would succeed, so they would never have to answer for what they did. Like a failed revolt against Caesar, now they must pay. They didn't think they would get caught, they outreached, then they got caught. That's what the public is generally led to believe.

However, given the levels of flagrant sloppiness, it is difficult to say that getting caught resulted from a mere miscalculation. More likely, they simply didn't think that far ahead because, if they had, they would have prepared contingencies. They had no contingencies and they left a highway of breadcrumbs.

What explains this?—Psychopath?—Ruling class corruption?—Drowning in their own swamp? A simple miscalculation or a belief that they would get away with it doesn't suffice. Somewhere, the Washington elite have gone off the deep end.

The impeachment campaign against Trump is a self-imploding, self-destructing, backfiring bombshell. The Democrats harm themselves with their impeachment proceedings so fast that news can't even keep up with the damage. Their resolve to bring their own demise goes beyond conspiracy —it's self-absorbed madness. No matter how much they can see how much they make themselves lose, they only turn up the temperature and lose more.

The moral of the story is that we should expect even more blunders as the swamp drains and the monsters who thrived there writhe in their last hours of miserable existence. Of course, that could last a few decades before it's all done with.

Cadence of Conflict: Asia, December 16

China is desperately grasping for straws. While German parliament is planning to ban Huawei against the will of their head of state, Chancellor Merkel, a Chinese ambassador sends a message that "there will be consequences"—when diplomatic channels go to the head of state, not parliament. The Chinese ambassador is like a dog barking up a tree; German parliament doesn't care what the Chinese ambassador says. But, in China different branches of government don't matter because that's just a "silly Western thing". So, the Chinese don't know how German government works because the Chinese presume that Germans lie as much as the Chinese do.

Moreover, the Chinese Communists have overlooked one blaring flaw—if Huawei isn't controlled by China's government, that would make it the only entity in China not subject to passive-aggressive threats under pain of organ harvesting. Moreover, if Huawei were the independent company China's government claims it is, China's government wouldn't be so defensive of Huawei being banned from Germany.

China has many weaknesses, self-contradicting diplomacy being the least. Its labor force is shrinking. Its economy is much more dependent on exports than America's. Its tech sector is even more dependent on importing American-made components. Tit-for-tat tariffs don't favor China in that regard. The Chinese don't spend as much on their military as America does, regardless of the hype from State-run Chinese news outlets. And, it doesn't own a very big piece of the pie when it comes to US Treasury bonds—the greatest liquidation threat China could make there is to offer a temporary discount price to willing investors. The cost would be China forfeiting any leverage it had by owning such a small part of America's debt, while America's economy might skip two beats at most, then nevermore.

Then, we have the anti-Trump camp. Many economists who haven't a clue where wealth comes from despise America's president. Everything needs to pay for itself, otherwise it will die in a suicide cult of bankruptcy. Maybe NATO shouldn't be in Germany, maybe it should, but the answer— one way or the other—will only surface if NATO requires Germany to pay for its own national defense. Bowing down to China may have made a few American companies rich—regardless of making a few million Americans poor—but it was never going to last long. Even though China took American money and started bullying their neighbors, those who profited from those greedy companies in particular are angry. But, most Americans aren't fooled anymore.

Trump played his cards well, and he's still got plenty of chips left to ante up for many rounds to come. That isn't good news if you're a member of the Chinese Communist Party, hoping to help the party dominate America.

Encore of Revival: America, December 23

Trump's popularity is soaring. The impeachment this week helped the popular president even more —well, if an "impeachment" that the House speaker chooses *not* to transfer to the Senate is an actual impeachment. In the words of Sen. Mitch McConnell, the House doesn't demonstrate much leverage by not, "sending us something we do not want." Not sending the Senate something the Senate does not want has made Trump even more "popularer".

Whether Democratic or Republican, everyone should think the House is an embarrassment to the country. Even Putin thinks the House is laughable. Smart Democratic voters won't want their politicians barking up trees, starting fights that help the other team. But, there is a danger— power corrupts and supermajority corrupts "superly". Democrats are handing the nation a supermajority Republican party by 2022, when the third round of Senate elections for Trump's tenure take place. That is when our freedom will be at more risk than it has ever been; when good people no longer have accountability they are no longer good.

Fortunately, while many Democratic voters don't value the Constitution that started the trend of ending slavery for the first time in human history, at least they know the power of gridlock. Democrats like checks and balances when they don't have power. That might be enough to save freedom.

Cadence of Conflict: Asia, December 23

China's in over its head. They got somewhat of a trade deal, though they never had much to bargain with because their economy is much more dependent on imports than the US economy. So, their trade deal can't have gone as well as they would have liked, so they were always going to be unhappy, no matter what they got. They won't be happy, even though they plan a signing photo op come January.

Beijing-rooted leaders in Hong Kong are genuinely confused about the public outcry. In all likelihood, the Chinese truly don't know how much they afflict and oppress their own people. Because they are out of touch with normal life—because they rely on inhumane means to silence any opposition—they probably believe dissidents are genuine misfits. Beijing remains oblivious to how cruel and rightly despised its rule is. Had Beijing even tried to know what real, ordinary people really, truly think, they might not have been surprised by Hong Kong's harsh rejection. But, Beijing never cared enough to try to ask in the first place. So, Beijing despises

Hong Kong, all the while doing so under the delusion that its spite is well-deserved.

The British have politely demanded that Beijing honor the 1984 Sino-British Joint Declaration and hold talks with Hong Kong protestors. From Beijing's perspective, this is as unimaginable as a Chinese demigod being willing to hold a dialog with a cockroach. Make no mistake, Beijing does not feel that Britain is making any kind of request; it is purely interpreted as an insult, like demanding one to kiss one's own rear end. However incapable Beijing is of understanding the polite demand, let alone obeying it, the demand remains legally binding. Britain is building a case for nullification and Beijing believes that every way out is an illusion meant to insult.

Then, there's Huawei. The trade agreement China holds no cards to oppose with won't matter. Huawei needs customers and Europe is skittish, to say the least. Huawei needs money because the Chinese government needs money. Central planning squandered loans on enormous, countless, empty buildings. The concept of "scalability" is foreign to the government that always gets what it wants, until it can't afford to anymore. Even then, the Chinese won't know why they can't afford to anymore because they can't understand "scalability". Huawei's losses will

weaken China's position further when it comes
time for round 2 of the US-China trade
negotiations.

Encore of Revival: America, December 30

The Trump trials are exposing what is broken about our political culture. Politicians don't know how to talk to people. They can schmooze and beat around the bush. They can use a thousand hours and a hundred thousand words to do nothing in a way that appears like hard work. But, they don't know how to talk to people so that something actually happens.

To a business man, the phrase "I need your help" is a polite way of making a request easier to turn down. In politics, asking for "help" is code for bribery. The two aren't at all related. When Trump told the Ukrainian president he wanted "help", he was being polite. But, the swamp in Washington mistook Trump for speaking their evil language of bribery. In psychosemantics, the term is "projection".

Trump's impeachment is purely along party lines. Statistics and figures agree. If you're a Democrat, you think his call to Ukraine was wrong. If you're a Republican, you think his call to Ukraine was somewhere between necessary and excusable. Any exceptions are marginal. This is pure party politics, which means that we can't debate the ethics of Trump's phone call among fellow Americans with any more success than we can debate guns, abortion, and redistribution of wealth. Now, impeaching the incumbent president for whatever lame reason we can contrive has been added as one more topic in a party-politics worldview.

Most rules that Democratic politicians object to are rules that the same Democrats created to use against Republicans just a few years prior. This new precedent won't be any exception. It might even come in handy one day, one way or another.

Cadence of Conflict: Asia, December 30

We are headed toward a massive inquisition of police. It could be known as the "Hong Kong Trials", where each police officer who served since June is combed over and evaluated for every step taken at every single protest, then tried under international law. It's not immediately around the corner, but the current powers governing Hong Kong are doing everything they can to make that day inevitable.

Over the holidays, neither protestors nor police took a break, except for a brief moment on Christmas at midnight, when protestors were the adults in the room to pause for a moment in honor of something greater. Many had Christmas dinner away from their families, largely due to East Asian culture's dogma toward older family members. Authoritarianism generally drives away people who are self-motivated and take initiative, family being a least exception. Older generations in Hong Kong don't understand that. Neither does Beijing. This Christmas, many middle aged and elderly parents faced the question posed by empty seats at many a dinner table: *Do you love your children more than your desire for compliance?* To some extent, families will be reconciled in due course; parents who refuse will lose even more.

Taiwan had its own drama over the holidays. An accused Chinese mole, formerly in Taiwan's military, is being hung out to dry for purportedly recruiting more moles. Former president Ma is accusing the Control Yuan of interfering by questioning the judge who let him off scot-free. That stands to reason since the Control Yuan was effectively shut down during his tenure, which, unbeknownst to most, gave even greater rise the Sunflower Movement of 2014. As if Taiwan hadn't its fill of holiday joy, US Congress is now working on a bill that will formalize the US envoy to Taiwan as a full ambassador—requiring presidential appointment and Senate approval. That is about as close to recognizing Taiwan as a country without recognizing Taiwan as a country as a country can get. China won't be happy, but the Taiwanese sure thought it was a very Merry Christmas!

About the Author

Jesse Steele is an American writer in Asia who wears many hats. He learned piano as a kid, studied Bible in college, and currently does podcasting, web contenting, cloud control, and brand design. He likes golf, water, speed, music, kung fu, art, and stories.

Jesse owns various brands, occasionally teaches writing and piano, and preaches the evangels of Linux, Open-Source, and Jesus.

Poetry is code.™

books@jessesteele.com
books.jessesteele.com